WHEN A TEEN CHOOSES YOU

WHEN A TEEN CHOOSES YOU

practical advice
for any adult

REVISED AND EXPANDED

Joseph Moore

ST. ANTHONY MESSENGER PRESS
Cincinnati, Ohio

Scripture passages have been taken from *New Revised Standard Version Bible*, copyright ©1989 by the Division of Christian Education of the National Council of the Churches of Christ in the U.S.A., and used by permission.

Quotes are taken from the English translation of the *Catechism of the Catholic Church* for the United States of American (indicated as *CCC*), 2nd ed. Copyright 1997 by United States Catholic Conference—Libreria Editrice Vaticana. All rights reserved.

"Forty Developmental Assets for Adolescents" reprinted with permission from "Search Institute, Minneapolis MN, www.search-institute.org. All rights reserved.

Cover and book design by Mark Sullivan

LIBRARY OF CONGRESS CATALOGING-IN-PUBLICATION DATA

Moore, Joseph, 1944-

When a teen chooses you : practical advice for any adult / Joseph Moore.

p. cm.

Rev. ed. of: When a teenager chooses you.

Includes bibliographical references (p.   ).

ISBN 978-1-61636-241-6 (alk. paper)

1. Church work with youth. 2. Church work with teenagers. 3. Spiritual direction. 4. Mentoring—Religious aspects—Christianity. 5. Confirmation—Catholic Church. I. Moore, Joseph, 1944- When a teenager chooses you. II. Title.

BX2347.8.Y7M595 2012

259'.23—dc23

2011046304

ISBN 978-1-61636-241-6

Published by St. Anthony Messenger Press
28 W. Liberty St.
Cincinnati, OH 45202
www.AmericanCatholic.org
www.SAMPBooks.org

Printed in the United States of America.
Printed on acid-free paper.
12 13 14 15 16 5 4 3 2 1

CONTENTS

ACCEPTING A CHALLENGE

You probably never imagined yourself as a mentor. But suddenly you find yourself in the role of spiritual guide for a teen. Perhaps you have been asked to be a sponsor at confirmation—a role that is becoming increasingly meaningful. Maybe your own child's friends or some young relative considers you someone who can relate to teens and can talk with them about their personal issues. Or maybe you work with the high-school religious-education program or parish youth group. Maybe you are simply a caring neighbor, a good person.

Your mentoring may be short-term—one or two significant conversations over a particular issue or a now-and-then encounter as the young person's needs emerge. Or you may be meeting with a teen on a regular and structured basis, as in a confirmation program or formal mentoring program. Whatever the context, this book is for you.

Mentoring has roots in Homer's epic poem the *Odyssey*. The poem's hero, Odysseus, was a great warrior who left his son in the care of a trusted friend, Mentor, while fighting the Trojan War. Over time, Mentor fulfilled his role as both loyal guardian and wise adviser.

Every adolescent needs a special adult to talk with, someone other than his or her parents or guardians, someone who won't judge or worry or repeat later what he or she said. Thinking back on your own youth, you may recall some person who fulfilled this role for you. Something attracts young people to certain adults and enables them to express confidential matters.

If a young person has chosen you in this role, graciously accept that fact and realize that you have something special to offer. They just want to put their hopes, fears, and questions into words with a trusted adult who does not have parental authority over them.

The "Understanding Youth Violence" fact sheet from the Centers for Disease Control website (www.cdc.gov/violenceprevention) explains that youth who engage in violence have a lower range of "protective factors," including connectedness to family or adults outside of the family, consistent presence of a parent when at home, and a positive social orientation.

The Search Institute's landmark study "Forty Developmental Assets: Healthy Communities, Healthy Youth" (see www.search-institute. org) describes the same reality in terms of assets and deficits. Among these forty assets that help young people grow up "healthy, caring, and responsible" are the following five:

1. other adult relationships where the young person receives support from three or more nonparent adults;
2. the experience of caring neighbors;
3. positive peer influence, meaning the young person's best friends model responsible behavior;

4. the young person spends three or more hours a week in sports, clubs, or at church;

5. the young person has empathy, sensitivity, and friendship skills and reports having high self-esteem.[1]

What do we mean by the phrase "spiritual guide"? Spirituality includes all our deeper concerns—concerns about life's meaning, our identity, relationships, and, of course, the place of God in human life. So a spiritual guide is not someone who only talks about prayer with a young person. We are referring to an adult who takes an interest in a teen's inner journey—namely, their struggle to grow into maturity.

"Spiritual direction" is a precise term that defines the role of a person offering support, encouragement, and (sometimes) advice to another who is seeking a deeper relationship with the Lord. Spiritual direction properly occurs among adults (and is to be distinguished from psychological counseling, which also has a role to play in total human development). Adults can focus just on their spiritual growth because they have already achieved emotional maturity—at least to a large degree.

Young people, on the other hand, are not yet emotionally mature. So their spiritual life is bound up with their continuing emotional development. That is the reason we use the term "spiritual guide" rather than "spiritual director" to label the adult who is called on to assist a teen's religious development. That is also why this book addresses issues of human development as well as spirituality.

A brief overview of the book follows.

- Chapter one describes teens in the contemporary world. Their culture is very different from the teen culture of ten, twenty, or thirty years ago. Their music and dress styles, not to mention their technological tools, are enough to scare some adults. It is a new and different world, admittedly, but kids are still kids and have many of the same fears and hopes we had growing up, perhaps even more.
- Chapter two discusses just why you are qualified to be of help to a young person and offers some pointers about being a good listener.
- Chapter three offers concrete suggestions for guiding a teen in prayer and spirituality.
- Chapter four explores the broad realm of morality.
- Chapter five offers some introduction to dealing with tough issues young people face.

The final section is for those of you who are responsible for setting up formal confirmation programs in your parish. This section presents four options for confirmation preparation programs: a meeting for sponsors; a three- to four-hour mini-retreat for candidates and sponsors; an unstructured, one-on-one program for candidates and sponsors; and an outline of a structured four-week, one-on-one program for candidates and sponsors. The teen who has approached you for spiritual guidance perceives you as someone who has something to offer. Trust that perception and turn to God for the graces you will need in the adventurous walk with a young person on a spiritual journey.

CHAPTER ONE

WHO IS THE TEEN?

Being in the image of God, the human individual possesses the
dignity of a person, who is not just something, but someone.

—*CCC*, #357

W e can all remember certain aspects of our lives when
we were teens—perhaps times of intense happiness
or of great unhappiness. But we also quickly forgot
a lot of what it feels like to be a teen. And, of course, we were teens
within a culture quite different from today's highly technological and
increasingly impersonal society. And so we will begin by talking about
what's going on within young people, what are some of the dynamics
making them tick, and how we can connect to them.

Searching for Identity

Psychologists tell us that we all pass through crucial stages between
birth and adolescence. During adolescence we begin to deal with
the question "Who am I really?" It's a time of defining our unique
personalities and what we want to become. But during this process
teens experience some degree of "identity confusion": isolation,

emptiness, anxiety, and indecisiveness. In our highly competitive and materialistic society, this confusion can be more exacerbated than it was when many of us were young.

Teens feel the need to make significant life choices at an increasingly early age; yet, at the same time, they feel unable to do so. They also feel that society and adults are pushing them toward decisions they may not be ready to make. As a result they can easily become resistant.

This is when a retreat to childhood appears as a pleasant alternative to the world filled with the pressure of being an adult—pressure that includes the need to achieve, to succeed (mostly defined in this culture as being financially secure and being "significant" in the world). There is a growing focus today on the plight of the young adult population in their twenties. Many are not pursuing the area of study they took up in their undergraduate work in college, sometimes because they can't find a job and sometimes because they have lost interest in the subject. Others speculate that this generation of young people feel entitled and that they have been spoiled by their Baby Boomer parents, while another theory is that the culprit is over-choice, or the myriad of possibilities in today's world. I suspect it is a combination of factors that has spawned this reality for what is called Generation Y, or the Millennials. The "quarter-life crisis" is another term applied to the daunting question they face: "What should I do after college?"

I have a niece who recently graduated with a bachelor's degree in marketing, and now she thinks she might like to teach English. Meanwhile she is working in a coffee shop. I have a nephew who has changed his undergraduate major three times, and a godson who has dropped out of college to find himself. The age of marriage in this country is moving to later and later in the twenties or even early thirties. Some theorize that today's young adults have been so programmed since childhood to excel and perform in academics and athletics that when they either complete or drop out of college, they want only to experience the freedom and relaxation they have never enjoyed. Today's economy certainly doesn't help matters, and perhaps this echo boomer generation, who have had their helicopter parents hover over them for so long, protecting them from pitfalls, just want their independence. I mention this phenomena to cast a light on the teens of today.

Understandably, teens' behavior can be inconsistent and unpredictable during adolescence. One minute the teen doesn't want to make a commitment to anyone or anything—and the very next minute he or she is willing to follow some cause or person no matter the consequences, or to make some rash decision whose only purpose is to have fun or to engage in risky behavior, or to choose a career without much reflection on why.

This can be a trying time for the adults involved in the young person's life, unless we understand what's going on. We have to brace ourselves to expect this vacillation, this contradictory behavior. We need to recognize it as normal and necessary and try not to take it too personally when we suffer because of it. We need some detachment from the inner storm of teens. Otherwise we can easily be swept into turmoil ourselves. Then we can't be much help to either ourselves or them.

Because this task of discovering "who I am" can be frightening, calling for openness and intimacy, some teens use avoidance techniques—what psychologists call "defenses." Some common defenses include alcohol or other drug use (and abuse); excessive absorption in television, music, or social networking, and withdrawing or isolating oneself from friends and society; role assumption—perhaps assuming a style such as emo, prep, glam, alternative, goth, gangsta, jock—rather than discovering one's authentic self; promiscuity or sexual experimentation; and rebellious attitudes and behaviors. All of these "defenses" are nothing more than avoidance techniques that seemingly take the pressure off teens in their pursuit of their own genuine self-discovery. Unfortunately, these defenses also tend to reinforce and aggravate teens' present state of confusion.

As adults we need to point out to young people the behavior we observe, label it, and challenge them to confront the crucial task of identity formation despite all distractions to the contrary. During this time of identity crisis we need to be understanding, yet we need to be ourselves and stick to our own tasks, life choices, and values. We can be most helpful by being good listeners (we'll talk more about that in chapter two). It's even more helpful when we don't judge but rather allow young people to come to their own decisions—temporary as they may be. (Of course, this is much easier for adults who are not their parents.)

Adam came to me one day and asked my advice about having sexual intercourse on the night of his prom. My first temptation was to scream, "Don't!" But I caught myself when I realized that he had obviously chosen me because he felt safe enough with me to discuss this very personal matter. He also probably was feeling ambivalent about the prospect and was clearly looking for some adult guidance. But if I immediately moralized or yelled at him or made a pronouncement, he would probably pay little attention to what I had to say. I also had the luxury of not being his parent. If I had been his parent, I would not have been able to be so detached and I would have had to clearly let him know he needed to be abstinent.

So I bit my tongue. I listened patiently to all the pros and cons he presented and tried not to judge. In this way I was able to reinforce all his own negative feelings about such an action and, simply by agreeing with the objections he himself was presenting, to support him in his struggle to live a moral Christian life. When he was all through speaking, then I was able to tell Adam that I thought he knew the right thing to do, that I knew him and believed his deep-down values were good. I think that at his deepest level he knew that to have sex would be wrong and harmful to this relationship, present many undesirable risks, and also be against the wise teachings of the Church. I was confident he would do the moral thing, and I admitted I felt honored that he had trusted me with this very personal matter.

This is what I mean by nonjudgmental listening. Teens need to talk about themselves, to reveal their private thoughts to others, especially their peers. By opening up and talking honestly about what they are feeling and thinking, young people develop the capacity to handle intimacy, as in openness and vulnerability, which eventually solidifies their identities. This is how they discover and become who they truly are: through the lifelong process of revealing themselves to others.

Moving Toward Independence

Sooner or later young adults begin to withdraw emotionally from their parents or guardians. This necessary move toward adulthood is both exciting and painful for the teen—and can also be painful for parents or guardians. Consider these two reports from a mother and her teenage son. First, from the mother:

> I'm having a tough time, a real tough time, in letting my oldest son go. I mean it's really hard. He's still my little boy, my baby. I carried him within me. I nursed and nourished him and have been devoted to his every need along the way. And now he wants to break away from me and I can't bear it.
>
> He runs from me. He darts away from all the time I'd like to spend with him. I think he feels smothered by my love. Well, it isn't really love. It's not making him feel free. He feels caged. No, it's not love; it's my need to hang on to him. And I'm jealous, too, of other people to whom he turns to share his deepest secrets. He used to share them all with me. I feel very alone.

Then, from the son:

> My mother—she just doesn't understand. I love her more than anything. But she doesn't think I do because I don't spend any time with her and with our family. I don't know. I just have to be on the go. I find it hard to spend time at home, and I'd rather be with my friends. And when I am at home I'd rather be alone and listen to my music to help me unwind.

Do you think I'm wrong? Sometimes I do—when I can see a hurt look in my mother's eyes as I'm leaving the house again. I feel guilty. I guess I'm pretty selfish about it. I want my family there when I feel the need, but most of the time I ignore their needs. I never think about making them happy. I'm so wrapped up in making myself happy and being with my friends. I do care a lot about my friends. I wish I could tell this to my mother when she looks at me that way.

If we don't recognize this very natural struggle for independence, we will become irritated, hurt, or exasperated in our relationships with young people.

Take, for example, the issue of a teen's friends. During childhood, children take for granted their parents' judgments about who are "good people" and who are not. Teens may question these judgments and strike up friendships with people their parents disapprove of. This not only helps the adolescent attain some distance from the parents but also provides a chance to weigh and test what was previously accepted without question. Yet parents may experience such actions as defying their authority. Or they fear for the teen who seems to be running with the wrong crowd.

How does one, as an adult offering guidance, respond to the situation? The answer is not simple, but here are some suggestions:

· Perhaps most important, try to understand what is going on inside the teen struggling to become his or her own person.

• Unless your sense is that these young people are pathological, addicted to or using drugs, participating in cults or other dangerous groups, or caught up in street culture, don't put down the teen's friends but rather ask what your teen looks for and values in that friendship. In other words, help the person reflect on the choices being made.

• If you are not the parent, act as a bridge between parent and child. Point out that while you understand that we all want to be free to choose our own friends, parents want only the best for their children and have legitimate fears about the possibility of negative influences on a young person's life.

• If you are asked directly what you think about the friend in question, answer honestly and directly. Young people prize honesty in relationships perhaps more than anything else. If you are honest and open with teens, they will be unable to have anything but respect for you even if they express total disagreement.

Children are like kites that parents spend a lifetime trying to get off the ground. The art of parenting can be compared to letting out the right amount of string as the adolescent grows and emerges into young adulthood. But seeing the kite—their child—rise higher and higher into the sky brings both sadness and joy. Parents know that it won't be long before that beautiful creature will snap the lifeline that once bound them together and soar as it was meant to, on its own. Our own *Catechism* states it best: "By free will one shapes one's own life. Human freedom is a force for growth and maturity in truth and goodness" (*CCC*, #1731). By slowly and carefully letting go of the reins, parents and caring adults prepare young people for adulthood and its challenges.

As teens grow away from them, however, many adults have difficulty dealing with the event emotionally. This is most difficult for parents with their first or only child. Nonparents can often be more objective and encourage the reluctant adult in the art of letting go. But nonparents can also have difficulty. Any adult who has become close to a child—a teacher, a grandparent, a friend, a minister—faces the temptation to try to keep the child dependent or to become overprotective or possessive because it is so painful to see the child withdraw.

What we need to realize is that our relationship with them is not over—even though it may appear that way for a while. The ground of the relationship is shifting, and that shifting is necessary if we ever want to reestablish ourselves in a new adult-to-adult relationship. If we try to repress or smother this natural development, we run the risk of alienating the young person from us forever.

The Peer Group

During the transition to adulthood, the teen finds a temporary way station among peers. There a young person finds a sense of belonging and a feeling of strength. In order to gain acceptance by the group, teens tend to conform completely in dress, hairstyle, musical taste, and so on. Young teens need the experience of acceptance by their peers in order to solidify their sense of self-esteem. Later in adolescence, however, they will need to individuate themselves from the group, with a new appreciation of their own uniqueness.

Mobile phones and social networking become very significant during this period of development. Communication tools provide the teen with a wonderful means of flight from parents to peers without ever leaving home. They also provide opportunities for romance. There are clearly risks involved with using technology and we will discuss these later, but the fact is that these tools of communication are here to stay.

Another significant peer connector is music. Teens live surrounded by music, usually dictated by their own musical preference. Both the music itself and the movement it engenders satisfy a number of needs for teens. Music is one of the languages, or common denominators, of the peer group. Delight in the physical movement of dance offers a feeling of release from tension. Dance also provides a means of expressing both sexual urges (which are surging at this time in life) and aggression in a safe and symbolic way.

Dance forms today are admittedly much freer in body movement than they once were, but we should not be too quick to label the gyrations immodest. The whole cultural view of sexuality with which our young people have grown up is quite different from the view that prevailed when many of us were teens. My own parents would not let me watch Elvis Presley on television! If the way teens dance today bothers you, the best advice I can give you is this: Never volunteer to chaperone a dance.

Riding an Emotional Roller Coaster

Teens are subject to frequent mood swings. One study concludes that an adolescent mood of extreme happiness or extreme sadness lasts, on average, about forty-five minutes. Yet we know how such short-lived moods can impact the people surrounding the adolescent!

Environment has a great influence on mood swings in young people. The teen in school may seem to be a different person from the one coming home with friends. Puberty increases the base level of hormones. This requires various adjustments in the body and, in turn, cause mood swings.

Others think that the emotional breaking away of adolescence causes a sort of "mourning" or depression. As a counterreaction, moods of elation occur when new love objects or relationships are found. In other words, the mood swings of teens are related to the making or breaking of relationships either in reality or in their fantasy lives. Still others say that adolescents are pressured to take on the responsibilities of adulthood and at the same time are supposed to enjoy the pleasures of youth, and that this double expectation causes moodiness. Combine all this with the precariousness and fragility we all experience in day-to-day living and you will recognize the emotional intensity we are discussing here.

Whatever the cause of mood swings, the important issue is how teens handle them. We can help them by getting the young person to talk about whatever has him or her in its grip. When a kid approaches you in a down mood, just ask, "How come you're so dejected, so down?" Talking about it will make the teen feel better, or at least will demonstrate that someone is interested in them. Sometimes teens don't understand why they are feeling depressed, but they should still be encouraged to talk. That in itself may provide the key to understanding and lead to a lifting of the heavy feelings.

Just a note here about mood swings that may need a referral to a clinician for a mental-status exam. Teen depression may be more than that in certain cases. If depression comes over a person and lasts for weeks or even days and is not always connected to a precipitating event, such as the death of a friend or a move from one place to another, attention should be paid. If the depression is accompanied by behaviors such as not wanting to get out of bed and go to school, suicidal thoughts, a loss of interest in everything, weight loss, or insomnia, it is advisable to have the young person evaluated by a mental-health professional.

In most cases, however, the mood swings are a normal part of adolescence. The young people who learn to control their energies and, despite their moods, move toward their goals in life will become confident individuals. Mood swings need to be recognized as challenges: The junior in high school who wants good grades to be accepted by their chosen college needs to study and perform even though he or she may not feel like it at any given time. Doing so brings a self-satisfaction that reinforces the capacity to take charge of life.

Our place in this process is on the sidelines, because young people have to do this for themselves. Our role on the sidelines is not to nag them but rather to cheer them on with the proper doses of encouragement and support. Life has given all of us hard lessons in maturity. We have struggled ourselves in delaying gratification to attain some distant goal or preserve a value. We have all put aside our moods and made sacrifices at home, at work, and in society. This is the experience we must teach and share with teens.

Psychology today has put a lot of emphasis on feelings—and rightly so. For too long society, and the Church as well, neglected the emotional part of life. But we also need to keep feelings, including mood changes, in perspective. "If it feels good, do it" is not a formula for mature human or Christian behavior. Moods and feelings will come and go. We need to help teens understand that the inner core of who they are as a person needs to be stronger than all their emotional ups and downs.

Along with the emotional turbulence, teens develop new reasoning skills. Around the age of twelve, preteens begin to develop a greater capacity for thinking. For example, they can start to hypothesize ("what if?"), form generalizations, and move from thinking in concrete terms to abstract thought. This expansion of the mind allows for the consideration of deeper questions: God, personal values, the meaning of life. But it also brings with it the question "why?"

Adults can get exasperated when the young person who once accepted things readily now barrages them with questions such as "Why do I have to?" "Why can't I?" "Why do I have to go to church?" "Why can't I go with my friends?" It's easy for adults to lose patience with this type of interrogation or to view it as a challenge to their authority. As teens grow older, it's important that caring adults take the time to discuss the "whys" that young people raise. This type of communication helps them to increase their mental powers and, more importantly, to get deeper insights into adult reasoning. Why do we as adults hold certain values precious? Why do parents think that limits that they set are in teens' own best interests?

We adults have more emotional detachment when serving as guides for other people's children. We can listen more easily when we do not feel our own parental authority threatened. By absorbing some share of teens' negativity, we can provide a safe place for a young person to struggle toward independence.

Growing in Faith

When you were growing up, perhaps faith meant giving intellectual assent to the teaching of the Church. But today the word *faith* means something that involves the whole person as well as just the mind. It means relating to God in a way that invests energies, heart, and hope. When Abraham in the Old Testament is called the "man of faith," the Hebrew word is closer to our word *trust*. Faith is a kind of trusting, a commitment to the belief that God cares for us and will bring us safely through everything, including the curtain of death.

We are all in the process of growing in faith. Research on the stages of faith indicates that young people between the ages of twelve and twenty are concerned primarily with relationships—the "interpersonal," we call it. This is the period when people learn intimacy and when true friendship becomes an important part of life. It's a time to learn how to relate to people to whom you are attracted in a romantic way. Teens make a lot of mistakes in exploring this realm of relationship, but that is necessary for continued growth as a person.

The religious faith of young people likewise involves the discovery that they are in relationship with God or Jesus Christ. They discover that God isn't just someone up in the sky or in the Bible but someone real who cares about them and who calls them to trust. Just as the development of a human relationship requires communication, so does a relationship with Jesus or God. We call this communication "prayer."

In the later Middle Ages, under the influence of St. Teresa of Avila and St. John of the Cross, growing in faith was understood in terms of "stages in the spiritual life." These stages are worth discussing briefly because this part of our heritage still has something to offer today. They are as follows:

- Primitive spirituality: Prayer is basically me-centered with a "Gimme this, God!" attitude. This is spiritual childhood.
- Purgative stage: We begin to get rid of false ideas and see God as a person, a friend with whom we are in relationship. Teens also begin to see parents and other adults as human beings and friends.
- Illuminative stage: We begin to realize that God accepts us totally for who we are, as we are. We begin to get rid of our low self-esteem and to accept ourselves.
- The "dark night of the soul": We discover we can't control our feelings in prayer. Sometimes it is hard to pray and God seems absent. We begin to realize that feeling God's presence is a gift over which we have no control.
- Unitive stage: We realize that life and prayer are one and that God is within us constantly. It is a feeling of inner freedom and being together, connected to the universe.

Developing a Moral Sense

Linked to faith is moral development. How does this relationship with Jesus Christ impact lifestyle, attitudes, and behavior?

Moral-development theory holds that teens have not reached the moral maturity to choose the right thing consistently, because their interior value system is not fully developed. Rather, they are at a stage where they are very concerned about group expectations. Their behavior is often based on what they feel others want them to do. This is not a bad place to be, provided the group is not antisocial or profoundly deviant in some way. But for most young people their group is composed of peers from similar backgrounds.

As they get older, they need to develop their own inner convictions about what is right and wrong and to act more from those convictions than from what others think. They also need to pass through a period when they begin to realize that moral issues can be very complex and that reflection is required. Despite the ambiguity of moral dilemmas, the older teen will eventually need to connect personal meaning, commitment, and responsibility to the choices he or she makes in life. As the *Catechism* states, "The education of conscience is a lifelong task" (*CCC*, #1784).

Another aspect of teens' moral development is that they are self-absorbed and generally lack a wide range of concern. They are sometimes deluded into thinking that everyone else is as interested in them as they are in themselves! This self-absorption can be accompanied by a kind of mystique that allows teens to believe they can do nothing wrong, that nothing is ever their fault, that blame is never theirs, and that bad consequences will never befall them despite the risks they take. (Sound familiar?)

We need to point out that they *can* be at fault and that they are indeed responsible for the consequences of their behavior. In fact, even though some behaviors may be the norm for people their age (as in "everybody does it"), the behaviors may still be morally evil and therefore sinful if freely and knowingly chosen. At the same time, it might help to remember that their cocoon of self-centeredness can make them unaware of the hurt they are causing others—as well as themselves. One function of spiritual guidance is to help teens realize when their behavior is negatively affecting others or puts the teen himself at risk.

Needing Structure and Guidance

The present generations of adults are more ambivalent in their own values or concepts of right and wrong than were parents before them. Uncertainty is not bad in itself, but teens interpret uncertainty as license. When adults say "I don't know" or "I'm not sure," teens often hear "I don't care." Our delicate task as spiritual guides is to weave our own values and beliefs into our discussions even when we must admit uncertainty.

Limits provide the security and structure young people need in order to discover who they are and what their own values are. Establishing those limits is the role of their parents, who need our support; spiritual guides should not undermine parents' rules by their attitudes. While teens may verbally or in actuality rebel against their parents' rules, at the same time they crave these limits and deep down realize that rules testify to their parents' love and concern. Of course, we are talking about reasonable rules, and we're not dismissing what we said earlier about the need for flexibility and communication. But the bottom line is this: Kids need structure and guidance.

Helpful adults other than parents and guardians don't need to impose many structures, but they still need to offer guidance and support to young people who may be confused because they live in a confusing and complex society. They also can help young people understand why their parents are providing structure and setting limits—that is, out of love and concern for their child's best interest.

If an adult in charge (and this is unusual) insists on unreasonable structures that create hostility and alienate a teen from his or her peers, you, as a friend to both parties, may be able to intercede on a teen's behalf and negotiate a solution. Sometimes insecure adults become overprotective and inflexible in their regulations. With another adult (who also cares about the teen) to bounce their fears and worries against, a parent might feel less pressured to continue a rigidity that only serves to alienate the son or daughter.

I knew a mother who would never let her daughter go to a late movie with her friends if it didn't let out before 9:30 PM. Since she was a senior in high school, I called the mother and explained that I felt this was separating her daughter from her social group as well as fostering resentment. My suggestion was that she allow her daughter to go but insist that she be home within thirty minutes after the movie ended. This conversation helped the mother feel better by being able to talk about the situation with someone, and she better understood the anger her daughter was harboring.

Of course you balance precariously on a tightrope in the teen–parent relationship. Never tell a parent how to exercise authority unless you perceive serious abuse or neglect. Much of how you approach this issue depends on your relationship with the parents. While it is true that some parents are threatened by a healthy relationship between a teen and a trusted adult, I honestly believe that most parents are looking for any help and advice they can get in parenting their children during the stormy years of adolescence.

CHAPTER TWO

YOU CAN BE A SPIRITUAL GUIDE

Through the exchange with others, mutual service and dialogue
with his brethren, man develops his potential; he thus
responds to his vocation.

—*CCC*, #1879

We are often uncomfortable being asked to guide another human being in the area of spirituality. Chances are you're saying, "Why me? I'm not perfect! What right do I have to guide someone? I have a hard enough time walking the straight and narrow path myself!" Sometimes people let a false sense of humility get in the way and conclude it would be wrong to try to tell someone else, even a young person, how they should live a Christian life.

But let's look more carefully and more honestly at why we shrink from taking on this role of spiritual guide—whether as a parent or guardian or adult friend of a teen. A good reason we may feel this way is that we think we are no better or holier than anyone else. And this is true: Nobody has any more of an inside track on God than anyone else does! This fact should encourage us as spiritual guides, not discourage us.

One not so good reason is that we feel incompetent in the areas of theology and spirituality. We are "just laypeople," not nuns or priests. "What do I know? I don't have a degree in theology or counseling." This feeling of intellectual inadequacy is a poor reason for hesitating to get involved in guiding a teen. Theologians are not what young people need. They need friends for life's journey, friends who might be only a few steps beyond on the road of experience and wisdom and the struggle to live in God's sight. And that's us—you and me, Christian adults.

A survey developed by the Search Institute asked Christians of all ages what they were looking for in the people who minister to them—in this case, this referred to the clergy. The responses basically boiled down to two major ingredients: first, an open, affirming, warm attitude toward people; and next, a faith-filled attitude toward life. The ability to teach, counsel, organize, administer, and so on were mentioned secondarily. Notice that the major considerations have nothing to do with professional skills or academic background.

Think of yourself. What kind of person do you seek out when you are going through a personal struggle? And think back further. Whom did you seek out for guidance in life or in matters of spirituality when *you* were a teen? What type of individual adult encouraged you in your own journey? Academic credentials had nothing to do with it, did they?

Young people respond to someone who they feel likes them and is not a phony. It won't wash, therefore, to say you can't work with kids because you're not "qualified"—if you equate qualifications with a certain educational background. If you mean that you don't like teens or that you're not open, warm, sincere, and affirming, then you may have a point. (Not everyone is drawn to this age group, and you need not feel guilty if you prefer to work with or minister to young children or the elderly.)

So the first "qualification" in becoming a spiritual guide is to believe in yourself. You can be helpful to a younger person just by virtue of your personality and by sharing your accumulated life experiences.

The late Henri Nouwen, a priest and author of many books about prayer and ministry, defined being a spiritual guide this way in his book *Creative Ministry*: "Ministry means the ongoing attempt to put one's own search for God, with all the moments of pain and joy, despair and hope, at the disposal of those who want to join this search but do not know how."[2]

Teen are people who "do not know how." Nouwen also said that a spiritual guide needs to be a "wounded healer," meaning that we paradoxically "heal" others by revealing our own "woundedness." For us adults to put our own inner journeys—with all the accompanying pain and joy—out on the table for all to see requires vulnerability on our part. So let's add vulnerability as the second qualification needed for spiritual ministry with youth.

Anyone who ministers to youth can awaken faith only by sharing his or her own faith. We are all attracted to people in whom we sense the inner freedom that we want for ourselves. By our association with "free spirits" we get in touch with a bit of our own inner freedom. It's a contagious sort of phenomenon!

Where does this inner freedom come from? It comes from two things: a deep inner reliance on God and a healthy self-image. One way to prepare yourself for youth ministry, then, is to grow in your own interior liberation.

Being a Good Listener

One of the greatest gifts we can give someone is to listen to them. Counseling theory teaches us that people solve their own problems (or at least get a clearer perspective) by talking out loud to another person about the things most on their mind. Good listeners function as mirrors that enable the speaker to see him- or herself more clearly, which then opens doorways to solutions or directions. Young people need good listeners as they speak about their issues, their concerns, and their relationship with God.

Here are a few simple tips for being a good listener.

- Try to pick up the speaker's feelings, not just the words. If you sense a young person is angry or anxious or depressed, say so: "You seem pretty down today; is everything OK?" Sometimes teens (and adults) are unaware of what they are really feeling; other times they are just waiting for somebody else to open them up by asking.
- Try to keep kids focused on what they are telling you without their going too far off the track. Sometimes excessive chatter is a defense against talking openly.
- After an event, situation, or problem has been explained to you, try to summarize what you think you have just heard. This type of summing up assures the speaker you have heard what was said.

Lisa once came to me in distress. A teacher had failed her for not turning in a term paper at the end of a course. I sensed that her hostility and turbulence were disproportionate to the event, but I let her keep on talking and vent her anger. She then wanted to stray off the topic and consider the effect of a low grade on her college plans. But I asked her to stay on point and come back to the issue that led her to talk to me.

I tried to sum up both what I had heard her say and also what I sensed she was feeling: "Lisa, I understand that you got a failing grade for this paper, but you have told me that you will still pass the course and that it will have little effect on your overall grade-point average. You have also said that your parents aren't upset with you over this failure. And yet you sound so angry and so full of feelings about this. Could there be something more to it than what you have already told me?"

I'm glad I followed the hunch, which developed by listening to her feelings more than to her words. I then learned that she hadn't turned in the paper because she had been hospitalized following a suicide attempt. While she didn't want a failing grade, it seemed better than telling the school authorities the truth. She had not only earned the failing grade, she had also shut herself off from concern and support. (This is a reminder that we need to inform parents when there is talk of suicide).

As much as we may ache for someone, we can never solve another's problems. We all have to take responsibility for our own lives. Don't let teens box you into a corner by requesting advice, because then you're responsible if your suggestion fails. Just keep throwing the ball back into their court: "Well, what do you think you should do?" This question helps people to get in touch with the solutions that lie within them.

If you really feel you have to offer some concrete advice, try to phrase it like this: "Well, this is what I'd do—but I'm not you." That way you convey your opinion without directly telling someone what to do. It is more effective to let people come to their own conclusions and then to concur when they have chosen good values or solutions. Let parents assume the role of giving direction and advice when needed; but remember that your own function in the teen's life is to be a sounding board, a source of understanding.

Being a Wounded Healer

As I mentioned in the last section, openness and vulnerability are two qualities that are critical to a good relationship with teens. Yet these qualities are often found more easily in younger people who have not built up the defenses so characteristic of adulthood. How sad! The older we get, the more open, defenseless, and honest we should become. We should become freer and freer with each year of life—and yet so often the reverse is what happens.

Older adults are often concerned with providing a Christian example to young people—and this is fine. But we don't provide a good example when we hide our faults, our struggles, and the unredeemed aspects of our personalities. Sheltering teens from our true selves does not help them at all. In fact, it inhibits their growth because it can generate a reluctance to talk truthfully to us, and it sends the message that admitting weakness is wrong.

If it is good for teens to open up about personal problems, doubts, and failures, if we preach that such openness can bring about real healing and deep community, then they have every right to expect us to do the same. If we tell them to share with us, we also have to share with them—at least to some extent. We do not need to disclose our darkest secrets, of course, but we have to be willing to talk to them about our own lives in order to help them get a handle on their own.

We even have to share our doubts about the movement of God in our lives. To do so gives the young person permission to doubt. We win respect from teens not by modeling a false sense of perfect Christianity but rather by taking the risk of laying our true selves in front of them and letting them see us as we are—belief and doubt alike. Herein lies the birth of respect.

This is one reason why adults who are still in their twenties are so popular with teens. These young adults are less afraid to share their confusion, their hurt, their emptiness. Because they are not preoccupied with being role models, they stand up to the scrutiny of contemporary youth, who generally have an extreme concern for authenticity.

Contemporary spirituality demands an unfailing connection between humanity and spirituality. We have learned that openness to God and to people are one and the same reality. We have to recognize that personal vulnerability freely chosen—so that our brothers and sisters might have life—is a fruit of the Holy Spirit. We have to discover that defenselessness is one of the finest forms of contemporary asceticism.

We have to help young people learn that, as Jesus said, it is truth that sets us free. "'God created us without us; but he did not will to save us without us.' To receive his mercy, we must admit our faults" (CCC, #1847). In his little book *The Wounded Healer*, Henri Nouwen made the following point: "A minister is not a doctor whose primary task is to take away pain. Rather, he deepens the pain to a level where it can be shared."[3] What Fr. Nouwen is saying is that if we can share someone's pain rather than think we have to take it away, we can help them enter into healing and hope.

Boosting Self-Esteem

Though teens can be self-centered, they still can harbor feelings of low self-worth. What looks like confidence is often reliance on looks, status, achievement, popularity, and so forth to bolster their own self-esteem. Behind many of those smiling profiles on Facebook and elsewhere may lurk feelings of inadequacy, insecurity, and worthlessness. St. Bernard of Clairvaux, in his treatise on the love of God, says that the first step in the process is to love yourself. How true this is! If we don't feel that we are lovable it will be very difficult to feel loved by God or by anyone else.

For many young people, the chief issue in life is dealing with their sense of self. If this is the case, your role as a spiritual guide is simply to provide them with warmth and acceptance. If you convey a positive attitude, their own self-love will slowly grow, along with their ability to trust. This may seem more psychological than spiritual to those of us who grew up in an era that compartmentalized human beings into physical, emotional, or spiritual aspects. But today we are coming to realize that we just can't chop ourselves up like that. Our spiritual and our psychological selves are so intertwined that growth in one of those areas is also growth in the other. To teens with low self-esteem for whom we provide affirmation, we are God's emissary, the representative of God's love and acceptance of them. Without us they might never understand this immense love that God has for them. What can be more spiritual than that?

C.G. Jung put it this way:

> That I feed the beggar, that I forgive an insult, that I love my enemy in the name of Christ—all these are undoubtedly great virtues. What I do unto the least of my brethren, that I do unto Christ. But what if I should discover that the least among them all, the poorest of all beggars, the most impudent of all offenders, yea the very fiend himself—that these are within me, and that I myself stand in need of my own kindness, that I myself am the enemy who must be loved— what then? Then, as a rule, the whole truth of Christianity is reversed: there is no more talk of love and long-suffering; we say to the brother within us, "Raca," and condemn and rage against ourselves. We hide him from the world; we deny ever having met this least among the lowly in ourselves, and had it been God himself who drew near to us in this despicable form, we should have denied him a thousand times before a single cock had crowed. [4]

Praying With Teens

One beautiful form of spiritual guidance is praying with a teen. A good time to pray together is at the end of a discussion, after you both have had a comfortable exchange. For one thing, it is easier to pray then than at the start of a conversation. It also makes more sense to sum up the issue that has been shared and give it to the Lord for his assistance. For example, when it is time to end a good talk, say something like this:

> Well, we've talked about a lot today. Before you go, let's just take a minute to pray about this matter. I'll start, and if you have anything to add please feel free to do so—but you can just pray silently to yourself if you prefer. Dear Lord, take Jamie's heart and flood it with your peace. Give him the strength and courage that he needs to face this problem burdening him. Help him know you are always nearby. Amen.

Praying with someone creates a spiritual bond that is really difficult to describe. But if you try it you will understand what I am talking about. You (and the teen) may feel awkward at first. Even if you are a little uncomfortable doing this, I would suggest giving it a try. If you take the risk, you will find that praying together becomes both meaningful and helpful to your spiritual guidance.

But if you are uncomfortable with this suggestion, don't force it. There is no use in making yourself a nervous wreck—better that you pray *for* your teen than with her or him. If this is more your style, at least mention from time to time that you are, in fact, including your young friend in your prayers. Just those words offer a real sense of spiritual support. You might even mention what prayer you choose and when you pray it. You might also look for an occasion to send a card to this young person expressing your care and your prayers.

CHAPTER THREE

TALKING ABOUT PRAYER

> Believing is possible only by grace and the interior
> helps of the Holy Spirit.
>
> —*CCC*, #154

T his meditation, written by a very normal and not too "religious" teen named Peter, indicates that we ought to take very seriously the possibility that teens can engage in deep prayer.

I have found it

I have seen it

I have been it

I was taken by it, and it and I were we

I was doubtful at first that it wanted me

I was amazed that it did

I was overtaken by its strength

I experienced a fullness that was unexperienceable

I realized that it has always been there

I know that it always will be.

It isn't until between the ages of thirteen and seventeen that the experience of God's peace is felt by young people. In other words, it isn't normally until adolescence that a person is likely to have a religious experience on an emotional level.

During the teenage years people begin to develop a relationship with God as a personal confidant to whom they look no longer just for gifts but rather for guidance and support. This is encouraging, because sometimes youth seem so self-centered you wonder if they are capable of letting go of the "Gimme, God" posture of prayer.

This means that as ministering adults we can talk about prayer as a relationship with a friend, Jesus—a relationship that has ups and downs and involves all kinds of feelings and needs and desires. Looking at prayer this way can help teens to abandon concepts of God as a magic dispenser of gifts. "What is the image of God that motivates our prayer: an instrument to be used? or the Father of Our Lord Jesus Christ?" (*CCC*, #2735).

Prayer can then begin to involve things not easily discussed with other people; it can become a sharing of intimacies. (We should note here that low self-esteem affects a teen's prayer. It can be intricately connected to feelings of being unloved by God, with the corollary that God could not possibly listen to his or her prayer.)

For all this deepening understanding of prayer, studies indicate that the major reason adolescents pray is still to ask God for personal benefits. The transition from seeing God as primarily a giver of gifts to relating to him as a special confidant is gradual. Indeed, we know that many adults are still in this very same process of growing more spiritually mature.

The early Christian community had to go through the same process. Notice the different conclusions to Jesus' discourse on prayers of petition in the Gospels. Matthew's Jesus says that the heavenly Father will give good things to those who ask him (7:11). Luke's Jesus promises the Holy Spirit to petitioners (11:13). Perhaps Luke's Gospel represents a more mature understanding of what Jesus meant.

Nurturing Growth

But for the spiritual guide the question remains: How are we to deal in everyday life with teens' questions about the effectiveness of prayers of petition? One way is to refer them to Jesus' lesson on persistence in prayer (Luke 11:13). More important is to clarify our own understanding of prayer.

God has a personal relationship with those who love him. Further, God so loves people that he is willing to meet them at their own spiritual level. The woman who prays for God's intervention in her life by lighting a candle will be met by the Lord in the way that she perceives God should intervene. God respects her level of maturity and deals with her as she is.

In the same manner the Lord can respond to the teen in the way in which he or she perceives that God will or should respond. Therefore, delight over a concrete answer to prayer is never to be minimized, especially with teens who might be enthusiastic about God's personal concern for them.

Unlike the person who lights the candle, however, teens stand challenged by a secular and technological age that poses hard questions about the activity (or lack of activity) of God in human affairs. Spiritual guides have an opportunity to help young people grow in faith so that their spirituality will not desert them in an unbelieving age. This is a delicate task requiring patience, love, prayer, and a lot of listening.

To accompany our young people on a journey of faith requires a great deal of personal interaction. Adults need to do a lot of listening to the teens' personal experiences as they work through the turbulent years of growing up. They need to review with them how prayer of petition is articulated, offer encouragement, suggest backward glances at their experiences, and help them reshape their prayer in terms that are more mature.

Schoolwork might be a good place to start. If a boy, for example, tells you he blames God for not helping him pass an exam, you might take advantage of the moment to ask some searching questions.

- Is it really God's failure? Did the boy study as hard as he should have? You can explain that prayer is not a substitute for action; we must work toward human solutions of the same things that we are praying about.
- What is the real need? Is this one test the issue, or is it an attitude toward study that needs a conversion? Does nervousness inhibit him; is it really peace of mind during exams that is his deeper need? Does he need more self-discipline? Can he use this failure to learn about his real human need? God is interested in his total development as a person. Perhaps that should be the focus of his next prayer.

By reflecting with adolescents on the nature of their prayer, adults can make brief remarks that can help expand the horizon of how to pray and for what.

Prayer does not change God; it changes the one who offers it. Young people might at first hear this truth as an adult's way of skirting the question "Does God really answer prayer?" But indeed it is not. Persons who have persisted in prayer of petition have experienced this even though they may not be able to articulate the change that has occurred within them.

To persist in asking the Lord to help in the face of an "unanswered" prayer is to go on a spiritual adventure. It is to be swept into a deep, profound awareness that the Lord clings so close to us at all times in all situations that we never need to be afraid of anything, including the experience of death. In the words of the psalmist:

A thousand may fall at your side,
ten thousand at your right hand,
but it will not come near you. (Psalm 91:7)

In other words, faith insists we have nothing to fear. Walking through life trying to be a good person, making decisions about our life as best we can, we should be confident that the Lord will care for us, be close to us, see us through all the difficulties we encounter. The kingdom of God is within us. To discover this reality is to understand Jesus' promise. "Ask, and it will be given you; search, and you will find" (Luke 11:9).

It is this profound discovery that we want for young people. In order to lead them to it, we should challenge some of their childish thinking. More significantly, we must encourage them to plunge deeper and deeper into prayer so that the Spirit can lead them to insights that will sustain them throughout their adult lives. Within this process lies the transition from expecting "good things" to the deeper, more lasting expectation of the Holy Spirit, God's own unyielding care for us.

Getting Practical

1. *Keep it simple.* Sometimes when we try to explain spirituality or suggest methods of prayer to young people, we intimidate them without realizing it. Affirm their own methods of prayer, what works for them. Don't encumber them with a lot of information; you might make them feel a relationship with the Lord is only for the chosen few.

Simplicity is at the heart of spirituality in a world where we are constantly overstimulated by media and telecommunications. This doesn't mean we can naively ignore the complexities of our day. It does mean that, amid the complexity and noise, the depersonalization of our society, and materialistic values, we need to cling tenaciously to our deepest human and religious values.

Simplification implies stripping away what is useless, harmful, or needlessly burdensome to our psyches, our pocketbooks, our time, our ambitions. If we are personally involved in such an ongoing conversion process, we needn't be concerned with being models to anyone, because young people automatically respect what is good and authentic and true.

2. *Discuss the youth's concept of God (or Jesus).* Is God close or far away? Is God warm or cold, concerned or not? Is God a judge or a vague reality, a parent or a friend? And where is God—in church, in heaven, in one's heart, in other people? There are really no right or wrong answers to any of these questions, but to ask them helps young people ponder who God is for them. You may also unearth some childish notions of God—as a sort of policeman, for example. In this case you can point to God's total acceptance of each of us.

3. *Suggest regular prayer.* Encourage youth to find a specific time to pray each day, even if it is brief. (Three to five minutes is sufficient.) Help them to see that any friendship requires spending time with the friend; so too with Jesus. That's what prayer is: developing the friendship.

Encourage them also to have a specific place to pray: perhaps a corner of the bedroom, facing a window. Some people find it helpful to create a "prayer corner" or place to pray with a special mat or rug on which to sit or kneel. (Lying on the bed fosters daydreaming and dozing—beds are usually not a good place for prayer.)

Lighting a candle or incense also helps create the mood or environment. (Make sure the fire is out when you leave the room!) Listening to music that has meaning for the individual, music that can serve as a preamble or background to prayer, can help teens unwind. But ask them to turn the CD or headsets off for at least a few moments of real silence. The prophet Elijah in the Old Testament discovered that God was to be found not in the loud wind or the earthquake or the fire but rather a soft whisper (see 1 Kings 19:12). In other words, to "hear" the Lord requires stillness and silence.

4. *Introduce new prayer forms.* Scripture is an excellent source of spiritual nourishment for young people. The Gospels are more meaningful than theology or doctrine and are helpful because they are so concrete. "The word of God is a light for our path" (*CCC*, #1802).

If a young person finds it difficult to spend five minutes a day in prayer without daydreaming, recommend that he or she read a short Gospel section and reflect on how it applies to his or her personal life. (A list of suggested Gospel passages you can read and discuss together can be found in the back of this book.) This type of reflection on the Gospel (or any other religious writing) is called meditation; it involves the intellect, the ability to think and reflect: "To meditate on what we read helps us to make it our own by confronting it with ourselves" (*CCC*, #2706).

Another form of prayer becoming more popular in our hectic Western society is contemplation. It is appealing because, first of all, it requires that we slow down and become totally relaxed, that we turn all our interior motors off. Our society is so geared to frenetic activity and achievement that it is hard for most of us to just stop and be still. Yet practicing contemplation is a welcome antidote to this hectic pace.

The most important thing to do in contemplation is to turn off, as best as one can, the activity of the mind: memory, imagination, and the thought process. Contemplation is quite different from meditation, which relies on the mind's activity. Contemplation is a simple attempt to be still and know God. It is the deepest form of communication with God because it is the experience of love itself. On a human level, meditation resembles two friends in conversation, while contemplation resembles two people who know each other so well that they can just gaze at each other without words and feel intense love.

Contemplative experiences can't be forced. Sometimes they just happen—for example, when we are overcome by the roaring of the sea or the beauty of a sunset. These are natural contemplative experiences. Here the effect of nature is so profound that we suspend all our thought processes, if only for a few moments. This can also happen in prayer sometimes—we can be so overwhelmed by an experience of God's love that we just bask in that feeling for a few moments without having any thoughts.

In the nineteenth century a holy priest named St. John Vianney lived in France. People came from miles around to go to him for confession because of his wisdom and sanctity. One legend has it that each day the priest noticed an old man just sitting in a pew and staring at the altar. Thinking that he was desirous of going to confession but fearful to do so, Vianney approached the man one day and said, "I notice you sitting in this church every day. Would you like to go to confession?" "No thank you," said the old man, pointing to the crucifix on the altar. "I just sit here and look at him and he looks back at me." This is what we mean by contemplation.

Generally this deeper form of prayer is a gift given to those who have been faithful for some time to daily meditation. I would not recommend it right away to a young person unless he or she is experienced in prayer.

5. *Recommend asceticism.* This harsh-sounding word comes from a Greek word meaning "to exercise." It refers not to prayer itself but to preparation for serious prayer.

Asceticism implies the self-control needed to shut the door and be removed for at least a short while from the normal confusion of the world. It means the self-discipline to turn off the sound, shut down the computer, and disconnect from the cellphone for a few minutes so that prayer can proceed undisturbed. Asceticism means that we choose to sit upright rather than stretch on a couch in order to be fully attentive to communication with the Lord. Asceticism also means we spend the amount of time in prayer that we have promised ourselves, no matter how many distractions come our way.

Diet and physical exercise are also ascetic practices related to prayer. It's hard to focus on our communication on a purely "spiritual" level if we have too full a stomach or are feeling the effects of caffeine or sugar or some other substance. The more balanced and nutritious our diet, the better our bodies will be prepared to turn to prayer. So, too, with exercise. Exercise tunes our bodies and clears our minds so that we are more easily able to turn to God in prayer. In fact, a good time to pray is often after a good physical workout, transforming the natural high of the activity into an opportunity to commune with God.

6. *Encourage journal keeping.* A good habit for anyone intent on a life of prayer is to keep a daily journal of the Spirit's movements that have been experienced in mind and heart. A journal helps us focus on our relationship with the Lord and can indicate areas where growth is needed, or directions in which the Lord is calling. A "nothing book"

with blank pages (sold in bookstores and gift shops) makes a good journal. A journal can be kept online, too.

If your teen is willing to share what he or she has written (or at least part of it), it can serve as a springboard to your session together. What is written in the journal isn't as important as that it is used. It's just another form of slowing down; it takes self-discipline to write in a journal every day. Young people who are growing and changing so quickly can trace their progress over the past year or even the past few months by rereading the pages of their spiritual journal.

7. *Define genuine religious experience.* Sometimes certain phenomena are mistaken by youth as "spiritual experiences"—the sense of calm induced by marijuana or other drugs, for example. If a young person describes something as a spiritual experience, and you don't feel it is genuinely religious, check out your hunch against these points adapted from *The Practice of Spiritual Direction*, by William A. Barry and William J. Connolly:

· Does it seem like a religious experience? Does it compare to previous experiences of which you are more certain? Is it consistent with what you know of God or Jesus, or does it just seem too strange or contrived or "far out" to you?
· Is it honest? Does it come out of true feelings? (This may be difficult to sort out with adolescents because they have such a jumble of intense feelings.)
· Is it characterized by a genuine sense of peace? Does it bring calm to the spirit?

• Are all the fruits of the Spirit (see Galatians 5:22–23) present as a unified whole? In other words, is the effect love, joy, peace, patience, self-control?

8. *Help prayer flow from feelings.* It is important to pray from the feelings we are presently experiencing: This is something adults need to learn as well. There is no right mood for prayer, nor should we artificially create one. If you're angry, tell God. He can take it, even if you're mad at him. If you're sad or down, then pray from those feelings; if you're peaceful or upbeat, pray from those. When we pray from our gut, we are genuinely praying as well as seeking liberation from any negative moods.

Previous generations had a tendency to block out negative feelings from prayer. Through psychology we have learned that repressing feelings, not admitting them even to ourselves, is not healthy. And spiritual writers today tell us that prayer requires being honest with God (who knows our hearts anyway!).

9. *Don't be afraid of doubt.* In a technological age, when we are answering so many of our own questions through scientific advancement, God's primacy can be easily overshadowed. Our young people are growing up in a culture that relies very little on the Lord; this is the society that is the backdrop of their religious faith. Coupled with this is another phenomenon: The crisis of faith, which used to be common in early adulthood, often occurs now during mid-to-late adolescence. *Does God exist?* This question usually arises from the more sensitive, reflective young person.

As a spiritual guide, don't overreact to this crisis. It is quite normal, even if you have never experienced it yourself. This type of questioning is more common now that faith has so few cultural supports, but spiritual writers over the ages have talked about this as a crisis that occurs in many souls. Faith, we must always remember, is a gift from God—not something we can manufacture ourselves.

If young people are truly seeking the meaning of life and ultimate reality, we just have to wait quietly and patiently until they are gifted by a new and more profound awareness of Jesus Christ in their lives. If they honestly confront their own inner emptiness, they will eventually discover that only the Lord can fill them up. If they honestly confront their own unhappiness, they will eventually discover the Christian paradox that happiness comes from unselfish concern about the happiness of others. And if they honestly confront their own mortality, they will eventually discover that only in Christ is there victory over death.

Usually, children return eventually to the religious values with which they were raised. They may drift for a while away from the faith community and from participation in the Eucharist and other forms of prayer. They may even do this in a rebellious way. The best thing we adults can do during this time is to be good sounding boards and listen to their doubts and concerns. We also can be patient with their alienation and not take it personally. And we can pray for them.

Talking About Sunday Liturgy

Young teens often oppose attendance at Mass as a way of testing parental limits. Discerning the difference between this testing and an older youth or teen in a real crisis of faith can be difficult. Pressuring the latter to attend could harm spiritual growth rather than help it. Following are some possible directions to take with the question.

- No matter how much you disagree, try to listen patiently to a teen's objection. Feeling heard is half the issue. In the area of faith, we need to show deep respect for another's viewpoint even if the other is young. We can't ever lose sight of the fact that Jesus' entire message is an invitation, not a command—and we need to reflect his attitude.

- Offer a challenge if you feel it appropriate. Ask what the teen contributes to improve parish liturgy. Has he sought out a more meaningful liturgy at another parish? If she wants to worship God on her own, how does she plan to do that? Remember that harshness may alienate someone totally; be very sensitive in this area.

- Explore parish opportunities for teens to work on the liturgy with other people their age to render it more meaningful to them.

- Realize that most spiritual formation occurs in the family. Most teens learn religious practices in the home and, if they reject them for a time, there is a high probability that they will readopt them in the future. If you are not the parent of the teen you are guiding, there may be little you can do regarding Sunday church attendance. Leave it to God and don't be personally distressed and aggravated. In many Catholic homes today, regular attendance at Sunday Eucharist is not a value. Maybe you could invite the young person to attend with you or arrange for them to get a ride to church with the family of one of their peers.

- Share your reasons for attending Mass. "The Sunday celebration of the Lord's Day and his Eucharist is at the heart of the Church's life" (*CCC*, #2177). The Eucharist is one of the most precious gifts Jesus left us. Your own appreciation of that gift will say more to young people than your words will. When the rich young man refused to follow him, Jesus did not coerce him (see Mark 10:17–23). We must always remember that Jesus is our model for inviting young men and women to follow him.

Distractions From the Inner Journey

We will conclude our discussion of prayer with a short reflection on technology. Let's begin by accepting that technology is here to stay. When I taught a course on ecumenism many years ago, we had visited various faith communities, and I will never forget a Quaker meeting I attended during the course of those visits.

An elderly man stood up at the meeting to share a thought. He saw the advent of the automobile, which happened during his lifetime, as the destruction of the contemplative life. He remarked how riding on a horse or in a horse-driven carriage, or even walking, helped a person to take in the sky, the treetops, the beauty of nature that reflected God. He felt that whizzing by nature in cars had destroyed our contemplative nature.

I mention this incident because I hear a parallel concern today about technological advances. I have twenty nieces and nephews. Last Thanksgiving, after the meal, we went into a large family room. All of them over the age of twelve were on a device at that point: laptops, cellphones, a Kindle, a notebook. Their parents and I continued to chat, and occasionally one of the kids would chime in. Finally one of my sisters ordered her children to "put those things away and communicate with us." "But we are communicating," my nephew retorted. "You just don't get it."

So what about this phenomenon of constant texting, social networking, never letting go of the cellphone, and so on? Is it enhancing the interaction among ourselves as human beings, or is it leading to less capacity to communicate? Data indicates that the number of texts a teen sends daily grows every year. It is rude in the mind of adults to answer a cellphone during a conversation, yet teens would see it as rude not to answer it. Is it just a difference of perspective?

Like the old man who felt that cars destroyed contemplation, some would argue that our technological advances are limiting the young mind's capacity to reason, to solve problems, and to appreciate process. Many Americans own a mobile device and use a computer in some way. Many report feeling stress if they do not have immediate access to their cellphone or the Internet. Clearly, technology is not going away. So what are we to do?

We need to develop courtesies, standards, and protocols as we have done with respect to the automobile. Over the years we have developed a system appropriate to the operation of a motor vehicle. We have installed crosswalks that call for deference to pedestrians. We have instituted laws about driving intoxicated, wearing seatbelts, and having airbags and other protective devices. We know how helpful owning a car can be, but we are also aware of its dangers.

At this point in time, we are still in the infancy of the Internet and technological advances in communications. We may rush to enact the courtesies, ethics, and protections that would govern a civilized and reasonable use of technology, but the advances seem to constantly outdistance us. So, in the here and now, what are we to do about guiding our teens? I have a few suggestions.

- Accept the technological revolution in communications and understand that texting and social networking are extremely important to young people. Remind yourself that adolescence is focused on acceptance within a peer group and that separation from the family is normal to some degree.
- Counsel teens to be careful about sharing personal information online and teach them how to ensure greater safety on websites.
- Remind them that misunderstandings can easily occur when people talk through e-mail, texts, and social networking. If 90 percent of human communication is nonverbal and occurs through facial expression, voice intonation, posture, and so on, then much is missed when communication does not happen in person. In particular, having an argument without being present to someone can precipitate misunderstandings. Teach them that that whatever is texted or emailed can never be retracted. We use to say, "Think before you speak"; now we need to also say, "Think before you write."
- Addiction to the Internet or social networking is a very real possibility. Keep young people mindful of this danger. Disturbing one's sleep to use a mobile device or computer during the night is one sign of this potential dependency.

- Help teens to understand that the most profound human communication can occur only in person, when all of the senses are involved. Let them know that there is no substitute for the happiness that close relationships bring. Encourage them to be respectful of their parents and older adults, who were not raised in this technological age. Texting while talking may be experienced by that generation as rude, as not caring about what is being said.
- Finally, encourage young people to spend good family time, good friendship time, and good time with God in prayer by turning away from electronics for significant intervals.

CHAPTER FOUR

TALKING ABOUT MORALITY

orality is a word that is often misunderstood. Many people see it as synonymous with a certain standard of sexual behavior; others relate it to honesty in business dealings. Both of these interpretations are very limited in scope.

Perhaps newer words are needed to express a broader range of right and wrong behavior. The words *moral* and *immoral* refer to inner attitudes as well as to external behavior. The feeling of love in our hearts or the intellectual idea of love is not enough. Love must be translated from feeling and thinking into concrete action in order to be real and credible. Love is not only an interior disposition; it is action with and for others. It is precisely this action that is the living out of Christianity by following Jesus Christ's way of life.

Popular songs contain beautiful lyrics about the nature of love. But if love remains within us like the lyrics of a song and never gets translated into action, then our love is empty and meaningless. As Scripture puts it:

> What good is it, my brothers and sisters, if you say you have faith but do not have works? Can faith save you? If a brother or sister is naked and lacks daily food, and one of you says to

them, "Go in peace; keep warm and eat your fill," and yet you do not supply their bodily needs, what is the good of that? So faith by itself, if it has no works, is dead. (James 2:14–17)

Action and behavior are the proof of love, beyond words and thoughts and feelings. A person can be said to live a "moral" life if he or she is really trying to put love (and all that word encompasses) into practice. Immorality is basically a refusal to care about others; it is selfishness. It can take the form of unloving sexual behavior or dishonesty in business dealings, but it has a thousand other faces, such as failure to share one's material goods or refusal to communicate within the family.

Forming Conscience

Conscience, as some of us were taught, is the "little voice" within us that distinguishes right from wrong, moral from immoral. Guilt is its by-product when we have chosen a wrong attitude or action.

As we mature, our understanding of conscience needs to mature. A more adult way to understand this psychological/spiritual dimension of our personalities is to think of conscience as a "developed sensitivity" or a "willing awareness." It means that we keep ourselves open and allow the gospel message of love to flood our entire being. It means that we keep before our mind's eye Jesus' command to love our neighbor as ourselves.

When we choose not to block this commandment from our conscious awareness and to allow the needs of others to affect us at an emotionally healthy level, we begin to develop a mature Christian conscience. "Conscience is man's most secret core, and his sanctuary.

There he is alone with God whose voice echoes in his depths" (*CCC*, #1795).

Having a mature Christian conscience means that we try to see the world with the eyes of Jesus Christ and to keep alive within us an attitude of compassion and gentleness. This is what it means to live a moral life. "Conscience enables one to assume *responsibility* for the acts performed" (*CCC*, #1781).

Conscience must be distinguished from scrupulosity, which is a minutely critical examination of all our actions that, in the end, blocks all action. For example, a person may be so afraid of talking about other people sinfully that he may scrupulously avoid *all* conversation about anyone, even when it would be beneficial for another person to be the object of discussion. The person who has a fundamental Christian perspective on love of neighbor will normally operate out of that love, however, and will sense when the conversation is becoming slanderous or cruel. His or her own loving attitude will dictate when the conversation needs to be quickly ended.

To help young people form their consciences or make a moral choice, suggest to them the following five steps:

1. Gather all the information or data about the issue being decided.
2. Get advice from someone with more life experience and who can be objective about the choices.
3. Carefully consider Christian tradition: Does Scripture say anything about this choice? Does Church teaching?
4. Seriously pray over the choice to be made.
5. Listen to the heart, one's honest "gut" feelings.

A person who actually follows through seriously on these five steps and is willing to accept the consequences and responsibility of the choice is indeed free to follow his or her conscience. And personal conscience is our highest norm for moral decision making.

But the process of rightly forming conscience is far more complicated than what is suggested by the attitude "If I think it's right, it's OK." The *Catechism* also points out that "the education of conscience is indispensable for human beings who are subjected to negative influences and tempted by sin to prefer their own judgment and to reject authoritative teachings" (*CCC*, #1783).

Recognizing Personal Sin

We can summarize morality as "loving behavior." To relate the word *sin* to this approach, go back to its original Greek meaning: to miss the mark. We can put that another way: Sin is not being our best self. Love is a constant struggle, and many times we fail to act in the most loving way because of our laziness or selfishness or weakness. We miss the mark of doing the loving thing; we fail to be the best self we can be.

In no way does this approach to sin minimize our wrongdoing. But it does keep the focus on our behavior and our struggle to be good people. It doesn't say that since we have sinned, we are evil people. Therefore, a good self-image is compatible with the daily struggle to grow and live—in spite of the fact that we fail so often.

Theologians talk about sin not so much as a specific act but as the drift, or pattern, of a person's life. For example, a husband who neglects his relationship with his wife over a long period of time, who fails to communicate and share with her, may eventually become involved with another woman. Not just the act of adultery but the drift this man's life has taken away from his wife is his sin. Serious sin is when the wrong that one does becomes so much a part of his or her life that it affects the entire being and turns a person away from God.

We can also look at sin as a form of saying no. We talk about committing sin; but another perspective—and perhaps a more significant one—is to look at sin as refusing to do the good that we could do, as saying no to love. We can also call this sin by omission. For example, it is sinful to steal from a poor person; it is also sinful for affluent people never to think or care about the poor and never lift a finger to help.

"Commission" and "omission" are the classic categories of sin. But modern awareness adds another dimension, which could be called "submission." By this we mean the unreflective tendency to conform to the norms of peers, national values, and the mores of our society. Some people seem to live like robots, always going along with whatever the crowd thinks and does. This refusal to take personal responsibility for our lifestyle and to make choices for ourselves about what is right or wrong can be another aspect of sin.

Being Aware of Social Sin

Still another category of sin can be called "transmission." What we choose to do in this complex society (the food we eat, the products we buy, how we invest our money, how we participate in government) affects not only ourselves but people all over the world. While we cannot be expected to master the complexities of world economics, neither can we in good conscience ignore our connectedness to others.

We are all involved in moral decisions in our collective lives, in the structures of our society. In the days of slavery, for example, many slaves and their masters were Christian. To many of the latter, slavery seemed moral as long as the slaves were treated kindly. Today we look back and say that society was caught in a sinful structure, perhaps without being aware of it. The very idea of slavery goes against Christ's teaching that we are all equal before God.

The equality and dignity that each person deserves is called justice; any social structure that is unjust is sinful or morally wrong. "Socioeconomic problems can only be resolved with the help of all forms of solidarity: solidarity of the poor among themselves, between rich and poor,...solidarity among nations and peoples" (*CCC*, #1941).

Racism is a sinful structure in our society; judging a person by his or her skin color is unjust. Sexism—holding that either sex is superior—is also unjust, as is prejudice based on nationality, religion, or sexual preference. And so when we examine our consciences to see if we have sinned or refused to love in our personal lives, we also need to ask ourselves if we are willing participants in sinful societal structures. For we contribute to injustice by our own actions, or by not speaking up when we should.

Dealing With Guilt

Guilt is the product of conscience; it flows from sensitivity to our failures. Guilt is often characterized by a depressed feeling—a feeling of dislike for our sinfulness and sometimes even an intense dislike for ourselves.

The first thing we need to understand about guilt is that feelings have no morality; they are neither good nor bad. It is not wrong to have sexual feelings, angry feelings, fed-up feelings. The wrong comes when we express our feelings inappropriately. But the feelings themselves should not give us a sense of guilt. For instance, the appropriate expression of anger should not arouse guilt. Anger is a healthy emotion; but buried inside, it can do serious damage.

Consider the story of Miguel, whose alcoholic father was both physically and verbally abusive toward him. The physical abuse waned as Miguel grew into adolescence and became physically stronger. But he was still outraged with his father. The treatment he had received bothered him, as did the way his father treated his mother.

When Miguel became involved in his parish youth group, he began to believe that hatred and revenge are un-Christian and sinful. And yet his heart was filled with such rage over his father's conduct that he often had fantasies of actually killing or hurting the man. Miguel's dilemma was that he had one set of philosophical values and a completely opposite set of emotions. He felt that his hatred for his father separated him from Jesus' favor. But Miguel's real challenge was to work through his deep anger with a counselor or trusted adult who could teach him legitimate ways to confront his father or to express his hostility in appropriate and healthy ways.

While we need to deal with our feelings to grow emotionally (and spiritually), we must also recognize that the feelings themselves are not sinful. Young people need to be taught this distinction and be challenged to deal with their emotions.

If we sin and act unlovingly, it is healthy to feel shame, remorse, and irritation with ourselves. Out of these feelings can come resolutions to change or repair our behavior and continue the struggle to grow in spiritual and emotional maturity. This is healthy guilt.

Unhealthy guilt lets us wallow in our emotions, feel self-hatred, get depressed. We indulge these feelings as a substitute for making concrete resolutions and taking steps to change our behavior. Guilt, then, can be useful, but it should lead to action and then be let go of.

Sexual Morality

The strong emergence of sexual feelings and the ensuing confusion these entail is part of what we all remember about being a teen. It's tough for young people today to live out Christian sexual values, because the culture at large offers so little support; in fact, the lure of music and media is very often opposed to a Christian perspective.

We know from various surveys and studies that most young people have had sexual experiences before they graduate from high school, and many of them way before that. We are seeing more sexual activity today among children in the middle grades; this is just the reality.

Teenage pregnancy continues to be a major issue. Also, we are increasingly aware that a good number of youth, in sorting out their sexual identities, are deciding that they are attracted to the same sex and are being more open about that. Traditional concepts of masculinity and femininity, along with the role of women and men in society, are being challenged. In short, we are still in the midst of a cultural and sexual revolution, which impacts the Church.

If a teen wants to talk about a sexual question, issue, or problem with you, consider yourself quite trusted. It's probably the riskiest area a teen could discuss with an adult. Despite their seeming sophistication, young people harbor many questions and fears in the area of sexuality. Here are a few suggestions to help you talk with them about sexual issues:

- Try to remain calm, not shocked, and open when teens begin to discuss sex. They are asking for help, so ask some probing questions if they seem to have trouble saying what they want to say. (Being comfortable with your own sexuality is the best preparation for a conversation of this nature.)
- Be accepting. Recall our earlier discussion of sin. Help alleviate unhealthy guilt by talking about God's wholehearted acceptance of us despite our failings.
- Give them (or get, if need be) whatever specific and necessary information they request. They could even need a referral for a specific kind of counseling or a medical exam for a potential sexually transmitted disease.
- Be firm in upholding traditional values. The long-standing and cherished viewpoint that sexual activity should be reserved for marriage safeguards commitment to another person and to the children of that union.
- Be realistic with regard to adolescent sexual behavior. (This is easier when you are not the teen's parent and can be more emotionally detached.) You have to retain a sort of "pastoral realism."

In the process of growth and development, a young person may very well have sex—and painfully learn some of the lessons that premature involvement can teach. Don't be too harsh on a teen's mistakes, but simultaneously challenge him or her to the high standards of moral behavior held by our faith.

It is helpful to know the distinction between abstinence and chastity. In the recovery community, "abstinence" means to stop using drugs or alcohol, whereas "recovery" implies that addicts have not only refrained from using these substances but are examining their lives—why they used drugs, what spiritual need drugs filled for them, and how they can become better people in sobriety.

In the same way, abstinence from sex has a negative connotation. Chastity, however, is a positive reality. The *Catechism* states that "chastity leads him who practices it to become a witness to his neighbor of God's fidelity and loving kindness" (*CCC*, #2346). Chastity is love of the other in the truest sense, where self-seeking (i.e., sexual gratification) is not what's important but rather the well-being of the other.

When learning to love others unselfishly by being chaste in dating relationships, a young person prepares himself or herself for the challenges of a lifelong marriage—or even for the single life or vowed life, if that is their choice. The Christian perspective focuses on true love as being present to the other and for the other.

A Footnote on Gay Teens

We know from data collected by the Centers for Disease Control over the last decade that young people with same-sex attractions are more likely than the general teen population to engage in substance abuse, risky behavior, and suicide attempts. This is in large part due to society's disapproval of the gay lifestyle and what we call "internalized homophobia," meaning an individual's internalization of society's hatred. Yet the Church teaches that "they [homosexuals] must be accepted with respect, compassion, and sensitivity" (*CCC*, #2358).

Increasingly, our society, especially among young people, is accepting same-sex attraction. The principle of abstinence from sexual activity applies not only for heterosexual or straight youth, but for gay youth as well. If a teen discloses same-sex attractions, tread lightly. Sometimes this is a phase or curiosity that accompanies sexual awakening. For others, it is the reality of their sexual orientation.

In either case, be a good listener so that the teen can get help to sort things out. Maybe they need some professional counseling, and maybe not. Being gay is not in itself a reason to seek counseling, but if the risks discussed earlier are evident, then it would be advisable. Often there are complicated issues like "coming out" as a homosexual to friends and family as well as the fear of the rejection that might ensue. The imagined or real lack of acceptance and the fear or reality of bullying are also indicators that counseling could be helpful.

We know today that we are not free to choose whom we love. We know that sexual orientation is not chosen. The bishops' conferences in both the United States and Canada have been diligent in developing a pastoral and loving approach to the homosexual community. Again, Jesus, who loved without bounds or distinction, is our example in everything.

CHAPTER FIVE

TOUGH ISSUES FOR TEENS

I n this section we will offer brief starting points to help you with some of the challenging issues of working with teens today. If one or more of them relates to your mentoring, understand that these brief remarks do not contain solutions but rather offer a direction for your own study and reflection.

Violence

We live in a world where aggression, impatience, and violence have become increasingly normative of human behavior. As believers in Jesus' way, we cling to the values of empathy, forgiveness, patience, and compassion. But the backdrop of our culture is saturated with violent images in our media, in our communities, and even in our families. Teens whose minds are still developing are severely impacted by this trend. The Centers for Disease Control reports that in 2010 a third of high-school students said that they were in a physical fight in the past year and 20 percent reported being bullied in school. Weapon use among teens is up. Substance abuse is significantly correlated with violence, as the National Survey on Drug Use and Health (2008) of the Substance Abuse/Mental Health Services Administration

(SAMHSA) found that almost 50 percent of teens who used one illicit drug engaged in a violent behavior, and that percentage rose with the number of drugs used. The National Institute of Justice, referring to the Youth Risk Behavior Survey (2007), found that 10 percent of teens reported being a victim of physical violence in a dating relationship and 25 percent reported being a victim of psychological abuse.

The reasons for increased violence among youth are varied, beginning with the preponderance of violence among adults in our society. Add into that mix substance abuse, delinquent peers, poor family functioning, and all of the deficits that can befall a young person today and we have a recipe for violence escalation. A form of violence we have become more aware of recently is bullying. Bullying is more than miscommunication or one argument. Bullying is a form of violence that is intentional, repeated, cruel, and targets someone less powerful. At one time it was the physically powerful who bullied the weak. While that still occurs, among teens today it is the socially popular with a heightened sense of self who are bullying the less popular, the "different," the misfit. While bullying is still done in person, much is also done on social networking sites. If a teen confides to you that he or she is being bullied, don't overreact, but just listen patiently. Encourage the youth to tell his or her parents and also the school authorities if it is happening there. While most teens think it will worsen the bullying, more often it resolves the issue. Also be prepared that there may be two sides to the story. Finally, if your young person is a target of bullying, some type of action in response is required.

Teenage dating violence is also on the rise. Females age sixteen to twenty-four are more vulnerable to partner violence than any other demographic group. Observe the dating relationships of your teens. Speak to them of warning signs such as controlling or stalking behaviors, isolation from friends and family, explosive outbursts, and substance abuse. These and others are early warning signs that this is not a healthy relationship and needs to be ended before consequences more disastrous ensue.

Dealing With Death

One of the most common fantasies in the adolescent mind is the anticipation of how others will react to his or her own death. A certain bittersweet pleasure is derived from anticipating the belated recognition of good qualities. Some adolescents think of themselves as immortal, while others dwell on their mortality. Amy, who is sixteen, wrote:

> The more I read about life's splendor, the more I see its tragedy: the fleetingness of time, the ugliness of age, the certainty of death. The inevitability is always on my mind. Time is my slow executioner. When I see large crowds at the beach or at a ball game I think to myself: "Who among them is going to die first and who last? How many of them will be dead next year? Five years from now? Ten years from now?" I feel like crying out, "How can you enjoy life when you know death is around the corner?"

Amy's concerns aren't totally unfounded. Alcohol and drug abuse, automobile accidents, and school shootings and stabbings as well as teen suicides have left few young people strangers to the reality of death.

Additionally, the death of a parent puts a huge stress on a teen, as does the death of a teenage friend. The experience of loss, however, is a source of growth and movement to a higher level of faith at any age if it is met with honesty and compassion. Never avoid the topic if a youth needs to discuss it. Don't allow your own fears of mortality to stand in the way.

Fears and Worry

In addition to fears carried from childhood, new ones loom large on the teenage horizon—mostly involving social interaction. Fears of speaking out in class, failing examinations, and being disapproved of by peers become pronounced during the teen years. The two major problems among both boys and girls are "making something of myself" and "the mistakes I've made."

The spiritual guide can greatly alleviate anxiety by maintaining an accepting manner. Being a good listener offers tremendous support to a young person. Also, of course, there is prayer. Remind frightened young people that the Lord has invited us to come to him whenever we are heavily burdened. But during times of distress, group prayer often works better for adolescents than does individual prayer. Because they are inclined toward introspection, teens' private prayer can turn into a period of mulling over problems, whereas group prayer can be a real source of strength and encouragement. It is therefore helpful at times for the spiritual guide to pray with the adolescent.

Even a normally hesitant teen thinks of turning to God in the case of emergency. The threat of nuclear and biological warfare, terrorism, and random violence in the street can be significant factors in shaping personality, even in the very young. Young people realize that adults are unable to protect them from these ultimate threats to life. The seeming inevitability of doom and destruction can render every endeavor and commitment tenuous to the teen. Uncertainty about whether they will even have a future has a subtle impact on teens' viewpoints regarding putting off pleasure (indulgence in sex, drugs, and an attitude of not caring) and investing energies in long-term enterprises (studies, relationships, goals). Teens simply find life's situations difficult to accept and churn with the question "why?" They have not yet dealt with the lack of control we have over this life. They have not come to appreciate the comforting thought that it does not add a single cubit to a person's stature to worry over anything, or that today's worries are sufficient because there's nothing that we can do about tomorrow anyway; we are in God's hands.

A word about trauma: In some teens you may notice that fears are irrational or out of proportion or triggered in ways that you don't understand. If a child has been traumatized by one or more hurtful life event (abuse, witness to domestic violence, intimidation, death), they are likely to feel unsafe frequently. No matter what comfort you offer, if you notice a heightened level of anxiety and hypervigilance, try to have them see a professional counselor in school or in the community to evaluate what is going on. They may require treatment for the trauma they have gone through to learn how to live with greater peace of mind.

Drinking and Drugs

SAMHSA offers information as well on current trends and statistics relative to alcohol and drug use among teens. It also offers suggested interventions. While statistics vary from year to year and decade to decade, we know that alcohol is a part of the fabric of our culture, and the teen who has not tried it is the exception to the rule. Marijuana use, which was declining during the past decade, is reportedly becoming easier and easier to access. As kids will tell you, "It's everywhere," and they are correct. A current alarming trend is the use of prescription drugs like Percocet (oxycodone and acetaminophen) being snorted by young people because it is easy to get and there is a myth that somehow it is a "safe high." These opiates are extremely addictive .

Marijuana (or "pot" or "weed"), widely used among teens, can redden the eyes or give them a glazed look. It usually causes a mood change such as withdrawal, lethargy, or giddiness. To "get stoned" or "high" means to smoke enough to feel emotionally numbed to the point that nothing troubles you. Marijuana use can make some people slightly paranoid; it can also lead to hunger in most. While there still is no agreement on the long-range effects of marijuana use, habitual use of it can lead to amotivational syndrome, in which a person loses the desire to make anything of his or her life. Marijuana can sometimes be laced with another drug like cocaine. Again, the SAMHSA website is helpful in providing signs and symptoms of drug use. Here are a few more pointers.

• A particular drug is not usually used in isolation. Young people experiment with combinations of drugs and often mix alcohol with some other drug.

· Teens have to know they will not be totally rejected if caught under the influence of some drug. They need a caring adult to review with them all of the dangers and risks, including criminal charges, that use can lead to.

The best way to deal with drugs is to be educated about them. Involvement with drugs (including alcohol) is potentially addictive. While some younger teens may still try drugs in a spirit of youthful flirtation or as a rebellious experimentation in defiance of adult authority, this is not the usual scenario. Most youth use alcohol and/ or drugs regularly for the same reason many adults report they once did: to escape the pressures of their lives.

Jimmy, who was living in a difficult home situation, remarked: "I smoke a blunt every morning before breakfast just to take the edge off my day." This is a dangerous state of affairs. The vulnerability of youth coupled with the confusion of adolescence makes alcohol or drug involvement potentially addicting. To discover drugs as a coping mechanism for life's burdens at such an impressionable stage can quickly lead down the road of self-destruction. In adolescents, the rate of addiction to substances is much more rapid than in adults.

As adults we must first be role models, particularly with respect to alcohol, the drug of adult society. Only "do as I do" teaches lessons to the young—not "do as I say." While we don't want to communicate a puritanical and totally negative attitude toward relaxation with alcohol, we need to communicate its limited value and that it should not be used to deal with life's problems. We also need to encourage youth to discover natural "highs," the sense of exhilaration in becoming a skilled athlete, developing talents to their fullest potential, achieving academically, working hard for a sense of satisfaction, and finding joy in helping others. We also should help them discover the deeper sense of joy and peace that comes from intimacy with Jesus Christ in prayer. Again, it's more important that they see us living in this fashion than that we preach to them about it. The way we deal with our pressures will teach them volumes about how to deal with theirs.

Coping With Divorce and Parental Separation

A tragic figure among contemporary youth is the "psychological orphan." This is the teen who either feels a lack of parental trust or chronically experiences the household as a place of conflict. Constant fighting between parents is damaging to a young person. Some researchers suggest that, despite the pain involved, it is better for the teen if parents separate if there is no other way to restore peace and harmony to the home.

Even though it has become a statistic that half of all marriages in the United States fail, parental separation or divorce is still a traumatic crisis for a child. It is hardest on teens. Why? Because just as they are struggling with self-definition, their primary role models shift ground. This can complicate the process of identity formation which we discussed earlier.

Guilt is also a problem. Adolescents may have an irrational but very real feeling that they themselves were the cause of the divorce. Another problem is deciding which parent is due allegiance. Parents often (overtly or subtly) press the teen for loyalty. This dynamic puts a tremendous strain on young people. Here are some guidelines for working with a teen whose parents are undergoing divorce.

- Young people need to talk about the painful experience with an adult who is not their parent. Parents are usually so caught up in their own hurt and anger, confusion and fear, that they lack the objectivity to be helpful to their own son or daughter.
- Encourage the parents to communicate with their teen about what is going on. They need to explain why the separation is occurring. They each need to be respectful of the young person's feelings for the other parent and not force them into the role of a go-between or into choosing sides.
- Young people need to be encouraged to talk with peers. In their circle of friends there is someone who has also experienced divorce. Many schools have group counseling or support groups.
- Teens need to know they are not to blame for the divorce. To be convinced of this, they may need the help you can offer as an adult. They need to be given a lot of time to adjust to stepparents or a new partner to their parent in the home. You may be able to help parents be patient with this process and not yield to their own anxiety to "make things work." As teens advance in years and emerge into young adulthood, their decisions about about holiday plans, the amount of time to spend with each parent, and so on deserve respect. The objectivity you bring as a third party can be helpful.
- Teens need to remain involved in their own projects, their own education and emotional development, and not be totally swept up in the divorce or separation.

• Teens need support and encouragement in the painful process of adjusting to life in a blended family. Letting them "vent" to you can be a tremendous outlet, and the perspective it brings can hasten the adjustment.

Helping in a Crisis

Teens in our day are less and less protected. Mass media makes them immediately aware of society's problems. They feel pressure to perform well athletically, academically, and socially—even from infancy, where there is competition for preschools! They must juggle time and schedules just like adults. Symptoms of increased stress include more drinking and doing drugs, more sexual acting out, a higher suicide rate, anorexia and other eating disorders, more runaway episodes, and more criminal behaviors.

Parents worry about the unstructured sphere of a teen's life, the hours when a young person is out on his or her own. At the same time, despite these fears, many parents are unwilling to invest much time with their teenage children. One study reports that the average father spends just five minutes a day interacting with his teen! Given these dynamics, we shouldn't be surprised that teens are often in crisis situations. And so how does the spiritual guide respond to such events?

First, let's define an emotional crisis as an event (or accumulation of events) where normal, everyday coping mechanisms break down and what once worked to soothe the self is no longer helpful. It is when you have to deal with a young person who is unable to regulate his emotions because of what he perceives as a catastrophic event or because he has been triggered by something or someone. To respond, we suggest the following:

- Respond directly, using common sense and trusting your instincts.
- Remain as calm as possible.
- Try not to become overinvolved emotionally with the problem— withhold yourself deliberately.
- Explore precisely what happened.
- Stabilize the crisis by doing the first thing that needs to be done in the situation.
- Refer the young person swiftly to the appropriate person or agency who can give necessary help.

Remember that in high-risk situations, where the young person herself or himself or someone else is in potential danger, you need to break confidentiality. Of course you explain to the teen that you are going to do so and why. While they may be angry with you at one level, at a deeper level they will feel grateful that you have heard their cry for help. You most definitely need to let others know about threats of suicide and you have a responsibility to report any mention of abuse to someone who can intervene. Always take a suicide threat seriously. (Eight out of ten suicide victims give a warning.) Don't be afraid to ask a depressed teen if he or she has ever considered suicide. (You won't put the idea in anyone's head.) If the answer is yes, ask further if their method and plan has been thought through. The more specific these are, the more dangerous the situation. If you seriously suspect that a youth is potentially suicidal, tell everyone who should know, their parent(s), and everyone who can possibly help. Don't get caught in a confidentiality trap. Also, in all of these situations where mental-health issues are involved, recall the adage that "a little knowledge is a dangerous thing." This chapter is not meant to equip you professionally to deal with these crises. It is simply meant to giving you a starting point for understanding some of the dynamics that may be at work. When you are unsure of the gravity of any issue, your local emergency room is the best place to bring a person for evaluation. If they are too volatile or you are worried about taking the responsibility of driving them to the hospital, call 911.

A FINAL CHALLENGE

In closing, I would like to challenge you, the spiritual guide, to examine your own image of Jesus, the image that you undoubtedly will convey to your teen. To do so I would like to quote Dr. Michael Warren, a pioneer in youth ministry:

> I have been concerned about the vision or portrait of Jesus being presented in many different programs for middle-class youth. This Jesus tends to be a middle-class Jesus, representing the dominant concerns of the moderately well-off and privileged. The dominant concern of the middle class tends to be greater comfort, and thus the middle-class Jesus is presented as the one who comforts. Overlooked is the Jesus who not only comforted but who also confronted and challenged, Jesus the *upsetter*. The middle-class Jesus is not the "man for others," the middle-class Jesus is the "man for us."
>
> If there is any challenge offered by such a presentation of Jesus, it is the challenge of accepting him as a sign of God's love for us. Obviously it is essential to understand Jesus as

God-with-us and as God's special gift to us. Accepting Jesus as God's love embodied is an important first step on the road to discipleship. Yet, to go no further is to remain with a middle-class and ultimately false image of Jesus.

The Gospels remind us in many ways that Jesus offers us not so much the Jesus-hug as a call for ourselves to embrace the poor and the weak and those who do not fit. In the Gospels Jesus continually calls attention, not to himself, but to the social situations that needed to be changed and to the people who suffered in these social situations, the poor.[5]

The most exciting thing about being a spiritual guide to a teen is that it is an opportunity to reexplore and rejuvenate our own faith. Young people have a wonderful gift for keeping us enlivened, challenged, and authentic. Undoubtedly their own questions and issues will touch the churnings of your own heart and soul. Try not to be afraid of this but rather look at it as an adventure in further Christian maturity. As we said at the outset, it's a journey together. As your teen grows, so will you.

GOSPEL PASSAGES FOR REFLECTION
AND DISCUSSION

PASSAGES	SUGGESTED FOCUS
Matthew 5:38–48	Who are your enemies? How do you treat them?
Matthew 6:1–9	Do you ever brag or feel "spiritually superior"?
Matthew 6:24–34	Do you trust God?
Matthew 7:13–14	What do you need to eliminate from your life to walk the "narrow way"?
Matthew 10:26–33	Are you ever ashamed of your faith?
Matthew 10:37–39	What form of unselfishness do you feel called to? What's holding you back?
Matthew 13:1–23	What kind of soil are you?
Matthew 19:16–24	Are riches your obstacle to God? If not, what is?
Matthew 24:37–44	Do you feel spiritually "prepared" to meet God?
Matthew 25:31–46	When is the last time you fed the hungry, clothed the naked, or visited the sick?
Luke 10:25–36	Do you ever pass people by?
Luke 11:5–13	Do you persist in prayer?
Luke 12:13–32	Is there anything you hoard? Do you share generously?

Luke 14:12–14	Do you do things for people who could never repay you?
John 3:1–8	Do you feel the need for a spiritual "rebirth"?
John 4:1–26	When do you think you have failed to recognize Jesus?
John 6:35–40	Do you appreciate the gift of the Eucharist? Do you receive Communion frequently?
John 8:1–11	Are you ever tempted to think of yourself as better than others and to put them down?
John 10:1–14	Do you rely on Jesus to take care of you?
John 15:1–7	Do Jesus' words "remain" in you?

This meeting (one and a half to two hours in length) is designed to ease sponsors into their role and to provide an overview of the whole preparation process.

For this meeting you will need name tags; sound equipment; a laptop and projector (optional); pencils and paper or a copied handout with the reflection questions and writing space; a copy of *When a Teen Chooses You* to hand out to each sponsor at the end of the meeting.

Greeting

The first thing to keep in mind is that the people attending this meeting may be feeling uncomfortable or insecure about being a sponsor. In addition, they may not know anyone else at the meeting. It's important, therefore, to help people feel comfortable as quickly as possible. Some suggestions are:

· Greet people as they enter.

· Ask sponsors to fill out a name tag.

· Offer coffee or soft drinks as people arrive.

· Begin the meeting on time. Delaying the starting time causes great discomfort for people already ill at ease.

Introductory Exercise

If the group is small (fifteen people or fewer), place their chairs in a circle. With a larger crowd, divide the participants into groups of four or five. Ask the sponsors to:

- state their names,
- state their candidates' names,
- tell how they feel about being asked to be sponsors. (The articulation this question requires will help dispel any anxiety about being at this meeting.)

Reflection

Ask the sponsors to reflect for five or ten minutes on their own adolescence and to recall the places and people they perceived as holy. To help them do this, play a song that reflects the changes we go through over life's journey. To enhance the mood, you may choose to make a PowerPoint show to accompany the lyrics—pictures of people from infancy to old age—to help the sponsors reflect on the passage of time. (For good suggestions of a meaningful song that could appeal to the older and younger people alike, ask teens.)

Then ask those gathered to answer the following questions individually. (The questions may be listed on a prepared handout sheet. If you wish, replay the song softly as the sponsors complete the exercise.)

- What place seemed holiest or most sacred to you when you were young?
- What person from your childhood or adolescence stands out in your memory as a holy person?
- What qualities did you admire in that person?

After five or ten minutes, invite the sponsors to share some of their responses with their group.

Instruction

Take fifteen to twenty minutes to introduce the ideas in chapter two of this book. (However, don't pass out the books until the end of the meeting. Otherwise the sponsors will be tempted to page through the book. Ask them to read the rest of it on their own.)

Break

Presentation

It is helpful to prospective sponsors to hear from a recently confirmed articulate young person who can help the sponsors crawl into the psyche of an adolescent preparing for confirmation. Points in this five- to ten-minute presentation should include:

• a brief description of the concerns of young adolescents,
• some thoughts about what confirmation may mean (or not mean) to the candidates,
• advice on being good listeners and cautions against feeling strongly the need to direct a young person's life,
• a short witness on this young person's own experience of the sacrament and the benefit of his or her own sponsor relationship.

Overview of Upcoming Candidate Meeting

The specifics of the next ten- to twenty-minute segment depend on what kind of sponsor-candidate interaction you expect. Below are three models:

• a four-hour mini-retreat for sponsors and candidates;

- a loosely structured one-on-one program for sponsors and candidates, using the suggested Gospel texts on pages 77 and 78;
- a four-part, structured one-on-one program for sponsors and candidates.

Question Period

Take five or ten minutes to encourage sponsors to direct their questions to you, a parish staff person, or the young speaker.

Closing Prayer

Spirit of God,

Spirit of Jesus present among us tonight [today],

give us the grace and wisdom we need

in order to bring our young people closer to you.

Help us never to forget that it is your Spirit

who instructs the human heart,

who transcends all our human weaknesses and failures.

Prepare the hearts of our young people to receive you afresh

in the sacrament of confirmation. Amen.

This mini-retreat is a three- to four-hour afternoon or evening program for sponsors and candidates. Choose an environment that is as warm and inviting as possible. If you must use a church hall, try to enhance the environment by bringing in lamps rather than using harsh overhead lights. Don't use tables except to do written exercises. (Tables create barriers between people.) For the closing prayer you might wish to use your church sanctuary if it's warm and carpeted. Set up folding chairs in a circle or horseshoe; invite those who wish to sit on the floor to do so. You will need these materials: name tags and markers, pens, or pencils, candles and matches, a crucifix, index cards, paper or copies for exercises one and two.

Icebreaker

The purpose of this ten-minute icebreaker is simply to help people feel more at ease. Set up the meeting area with back-to-back pairs of chairs. As people arrive, give them name tags, an index card, and a pen or pencil. Ask sponsor and candidate to sit with their backs to each other. Begin the meeting by asking sponsors and candidates to write on the index card, without looking at the other, their best estimate of:

· the color of their sponsor's/candidate's eyes,

· their sponsor's/candidate's shoe size,

· where their sponsor/candidate would most like to go on vacation,

• their sponsor's/candidate's favorite TV show or movie,

• a celebrity their sponsor/candidate admires.

When they are finished, ask them to write on the back of the index card two statements about themselves, one true and one false. Then invite the sponsors and candidates to turn their chairs toward each other and share their answers with each other and to correct each other's answers.

Next invite each pair to join with another pair (preferably people they do not know). Ask them to introduce each other by describing their partners with the correct answers to the five questions. Have each group member read both the true and the false statements about themselves. Group members should then guess which statement is which.

Exercise One

Retaining groups of four, pass out paper and give sponsors and candidates five minutes to complete the following sentences privately.

• An area of my life in which I feel challenged to grow spiritually is:

• One of the most difficult things about faith or religion for me is:

Presentation One

Ask a teen (perhaps recently confirmed) and an adult (perhaps someone who has been a sponsor) each to make a ten- to fifteen-minute "witness talk," sharing their responses to these two questions. These moments of sharing should really be *sharing*—not instructional, philosophical, or "preachy." They should also be as candid and open as possible; they should include details and personal stories.

Sharing

After the speakers' presentations, invite the groups of four to spend fifteen minutes sharing their responses to the first exercise. No one should be pressured to reveal his or her answers: Each person should share at a comfortable level.

Break

Presentation Two

Another young person and another adult each makes a ten- to fifteen-minute witness talk based on the questions in exercise two (below). The same qualities listed in presentation one should mark these moments of sharing. Be sure that both sexes are represented. The four speakers should not be all males or all females.

Exercise Two

Ask sponsors and candidates to take five minutes to answer the following questions.

- On a scale of 1 (very distant) to 10 (very close), what is the quality of your current relationship with Jesus?
- What obstacles (if any) keep you separated from Jesus?
- What is your hope for your future relationship with Jesus or for your experience of the sacrament of confirmation?

Sharing

Give the groups of four twenty minutes to share their responses and also to respond to what other group members say. Again, no one should be pressured to reveal his or her answers; each person should feel comfortable with the sharing.

Prayer Service

An atmosphere conducive to prayer is crucial to this thirty-minute service. If you are using a hall, dim the lights and put a candle, a crucifix, and a Bible on a small table or on the floor in the center of the circle.

As people enter, play a song on a CD or ask them to sing an opening song. An excellent mood setter appropriate to confirmation is the Taizé chant "Veni, Sancte Spiritus" from the Taizé CD of the same name or from *Wait for the Lord*. Invite the group simply to repeat the refrain, "Veni, Sancte Spiritus."

Reading

Ask someone to read aloud 2 Thessalonians 2:13—3:5 from the Bible in the center of the circle.

Passing of the Crucifix

Take the crucifix from the center of the circle. Say that you are going to pass it around the group. Ask that each one take it and, while gazing at it, pray briefly either aloud or in the privacy of one's own heart. Model the prayer aloud by beginning the circle with yourself or someone else who is willing to pray aloud.

After the crucifix has gone around the circle, return it to its place in the center.

Litany of the Holy Spirit

The response is "Come, Holy Spirit."

Leader: Into our world weary of war,

(*response*)

Into our nation needing guidance,

(*response*)

Into our families longing for healing,

(*response*)

Into our parish community praying for unity,

(*response*)

Into our hearts seeking your grace,

(*response*)

The response is "Spirit, give us strength."

Leader: To be witnesses to Jesus,

(*response*)

Not to fear the disapproval of others,

(*response*)

To be faithful when it's difficult,

(*response*)

To be prophets for our day,

(*response*)

The response is "Refresh us, Lord."

Leader: With your rejuvenating grace,

   (response)

With your body and blood,

   (response)

With your tenderness and mercy,

   (response)

With your comfort and guidance,

   (response)

With your Spirit which ever renews,

   (response)

Concluding Prayer

Come Holy Spirit and renew the face of the world that we live in. Let your blessings fall like the morning dew into our midst at confirmation. Keep us safe under your wing as we await your outpouring. Amen.

AN UNSTRUCTURED, ONE-ON-ONE, SPONSOR-CANDIDATE PROGRAM

Whatever the duration of the sponsor-candidate program, the twenty Gospel passages for reflection and discussion (pages 77–78) can serve as a basis for the conversations between sponsor and candidate. The sponsor should choose an appropriate number of the Gospel selections that he or she feels will elicit the most discussion.

Here are some basic guidelines for these sponsor-candidate meetings.

- Plan to spend twenty to forty-five minutes on each meeting.
- Choose a mutually agreeable time and place where quiet conversation will be possible.
- Begin the meeting by reading aloud the Gospel passage and the commentary.
- Encourage sponsors to share as much as candidates do. Sponsors' roles are to be companions and sharers of the faith, not teachers or catechists.
- If possible, conclude each meeting with spontaneous prayer.

The following material includes suggestions for four distinct one-on-one meetings between sponsor and candidate using Scripture as a springboard. The following directives apply to each meeting.

· Meet in a quiet place for forty-five to sixty minutes.

· Begin by reading the appropriate Scripture text aloud.

· Ask both sponsor and candidate to complete the exercise in writing and then to share their responses with each other.

· Close each meeting by joining hands and praying briefly in silence, praying spontaneously, or saying the Lord's Prayer together.

Meeting One

Scripture

"Blessed are the poor in spirit, for theirs is the kingdom of heaven" (Matthew 5:3).

Commentary

There are two ways of being poor. In this early chapter of his Gospel, Matthew is not talking about the poverty that comes from having no money or from living in destitute conditions. The type of poverty that Matthew says brings true happiness is a different kind indeed, for we all know that to be without material possessions is no guarantee of a joyous life. Perhaps a better word than *poverty* in this passage would be *dependency*.

We may not often think about experiences of being dependent, yet we have these experiences all the time. For example, if it were not for our alarm clock or a family member we would not have awakened this morning on time. Do we ever stop to realize that small area of dependency in our lives? Do we stop to think how dependent we are on the food that we eat each day to keep our bodies in good health? In our modern society we take for granted so many things that we are often not even aware of our reliance on them until the power goes out in a storm.

In this brief line from his Gospel, Matthew is talking about a type of spiritual dependency. Perhaps the key to this passage is knowing how dependent we are: Happy are those who know that they are poor. Some of us delude ourselves by thinking we are not dependent on anything or anyone. Do we ever stop to realize that we are?

Exercise: Recognizing Dependency
Complete the following sentences.

- Three healthy dependencies in my life are:
- One unhealthy dependency in my life is:
- I depend on Jesus to help me in my struggles ___ percent of the time.

Meeting Two

Scripture
You have heard that it was said, "An eye for an eye and a tooth for a tooth." But I say to you, Do not resist an evildoer. But if anyone strikes you on the right cheek, turn the other also; and if anyone wants to sue you and take your coat, give your cloak as well; and if anyone forces

you to go one mile, go also the second mile. Give to everyone who begs from you, and do not refuse anyone who wants to borrow from you. (Matthew 5:38–42)

Commentary

Under Jewish law one person could sue another for stealing. In these examples Jesus is rejecting an ancient Near Eastern custom of revenge. But we know that the Gospel was written for all people and holds a message for us here and now.

Not many of us are going to do the things mentioned in this passage. There are all sorts of ways, however, that we can translate these examples into our own lives. What about lending money repeatedly to a friend? What about running an errand for someone twice in the same day? And what about doing something or going somewhere with a friend or a parent, even if we don't particularly care to, simply to do what they want instead of what we want?

This is a difficult passage, both in terms of understanding what it means and in the challenge it presents. You can see from this brief reading that to be a good Christian requires more than just going to church on Sunday.

Exercise: The Call to Kindness

- Name a person in your life to whom you are sometimes (or often) unkind.
- Name an area in your family life where you could be more kind.
- Name one reason for your most common failure to be kind.
- Name an area in your friendships where you could be more kind.

- Name an area in your life where you feel Jesus would like you to "go an extra mile" of kindness.
- Name a resolution you can make for tomorrow (a specific act of kindness you could perform).

Meeting Three

Scripture

He put before them another parable: "The kingdom of heaven is like a mustard seed that someone took and sowed in his field; it is the smallest of all the seeds, but when it has grown it is the greatest of shrubs and becomes a tree, so that the birds of the air come and make nests in its branches." (Matthew 13:31–32)

Commentary

Patience is not a common virtue in today's frenetic society. All you need to do to realize this is to stand and watch people waiting in line. We are used to instant communications and the immediacy of modern technology. On an airplane or a bus that has arrived at its destination, disembarking passengers press forward as if rushing will get them out the door more quickly.

So patience does not come easily in our culture. The patient woman will often find herself standing alone in a crowd that is rushing about in a frenzy. The patient man will often be accused for his seeming inactivity. And yet, if we are to meet Christ in a closer way, we shall have to prepare our hearts quietly, carefully. To expect an immediate, deep relationship with the Lord is to make the mistake that our fast-paced culture urges on us.

Spiritual growth demands emotional growth, a great deal of human experience, much time, and prayer. Growth in human relationships—emotional growth—is a long process. Spiritual growth is also a long process, one that entails fidelity to prayer and to worship. The fruit of that fidelity is the coming of Jesus into our lives at an ever-deeper level:

Exercise: Jesus and Me

· Indicate the quality of your current relationship with Jesus on a scale of 1 (very distant) to 10 (very close).

· List two obstacles that keep you from Jesus.

· Name an area of your relationship with Jesus that confuses you.

· Name one way you know you could grow closer to Jesus.

Meeting Four

Scripture

Immediately he made the disciples get into the boat and go on ahead to the other side, while he dismissed the crowds. And after he had dismissed the crowds, he went up the mountain by himself to pray. When evening came, he was there alone, but by this time the boat, battered by the waves, was far from the land, for the wind was against them. And early in the morning he came walking toward them on the sea. But when the disciples saw him walking on the sea, they were terrified, saying "It is a ghost!" And they cried out in fear. But immediately Jesus spoke to them and said, "Take heart, it is I; do not be afraid."

Peter answered him, "Lord, if it is you, command me to come to you on the water." He said, "Come." So Peter got out of the boat, started walking on the water, and came towards Jesus. But when he noticed the strong wind, he became frightened, and beginning to sink, he cried out, "Lord, save me!" Jesus immediately reached out his hand and caught him, saying to him, "You of little faith, why did you doubt?" When they got into the boat, the wind ceased. And those in the boat worshiped him, saying, "Truly you are the Son of God." (Matthew 14:22–33)

Commentary

Let's start by saying that God does not usually contradict the forces of nature he has established. Therefore, this miracle must be considered a special one, meant to teach a universal lesson. The lesson, of course, is that of trust. Peter's problem, basically, was that he didn't dare put his entire confidence in Jesus' invitation to come to him. The question this raises to us is: How willing are we to put our trust in other people? Do we really believe that people care about us, that they enjoy being with us, that they love us? Or do we doubt other people and always ask ourselves questions about their sincerity and motivation? If we distrust others, it is usually because we have had some bad experiences along the way. Perhaps we once told a secret to someone and that person betrayed us. Maybe we once thought someone was our friend and that person hurt us. Maybe a trusted adult abused us in some way. After bad experiences like this, the human temptation is to crawl into a shell. But this leads to loneliness and isolation and increases our misery.

It is true that people sometimes hurt us, even people we trust. But we must be careful about two things. First, when people are inconsiderate toward us, it is sometimes because they are having personal problems. They may be in poor health. They may be in a bad mood. They may be jealous of something we have done. This is why ongoing communication is so important between friends and family members. By talking things out, we usually realize that we are still very lovable.

The second thing we must be careful about is our reaction toward life after we really have been rejected, after an experience of misplaced trust. One person may have let us down, but we cannot let that interfere with our establishing new relationships.

Exercise: Trust Barometer

· On a scale of 1 (not at all) to 10 (all the time), rate how much you trust yourself, your friends, your parents, God.
· In what area in your life do you wish you could develop more trust?
· When is it difficult for you to trust God?
· Do you see a way you could grow in trust?

1. "Forty Developmental Assets: Healthy Communities, Healthy Youth," Search Institute (Minneapolis), www.search-institute.org.

2. Henri Nouwen, *Creative Ministry* (New York: Doubleday, 1971), p. 116.

3. Henri Nouwen, *The Wounded Healer: Ministry in Contemporary Society* (New York: Doubleday, 1972), p. 92.

4. Carl Jung, "Psychotherapy or the Clergy," chapter five of *Psychology and Religion: West and East* (Princeton, N.J.: Princeton University Press, 1975), pp. 519–520.

5. Michael Warren, "New Stage in Weekend Retreats for Teens," *Origins*, June 1986.

Barry, William A. and William J. Connolly. *The Practice of Spiritual Direction*. New York: Harper & Row, 1986.

DiGiacomo, James. *Teaching Right From Wrong: The Moral Education of Today's Youth*. Washington, D.C.: National Catholic Education Association, 2000.

Elkind, David. *The Hurried Child: Growing Up Too Fast Too Soon*. New York: Perseus, 2001.

Gilligan, James. *Violence: Our Deadly Epidemic and Its Causes*. New York: Vintage, 1997.

Goebel, Jerry. *The Deepest Longing of Young People: Loving Without Conditions*. Winona, Minn.: Saint Mary's, 2006.

Ng, David. *Youth in the Community of Disciples*. Valley Forge, Pa.: Judson, 2004.

Sadler, Katharine. *What Adults Need to Know About Kids and Substance Use: Dealing with Alcohol, Tobacco, and Other Drugs*. Minneapolis: Search Institute, 2011.

Sawyer, Kieran, *Sex and the Teenager: Choices and Decisions*. Notre Dame, Ind.: Ave Maria, 2008.

Vogt, Brandon. *The Church and the New Media: Engaging the Digital Revolution*. Huntington, Ind.: Our Sunday Visitor, 2011.

ABOUT THE AUTHOR

Joseph Moore holds master's degrees in both religious studies and counseling. He counsels young people involved in the criminal justice system and directs a mentoring program for at-risk teenagers at Catholic Charities in Brockton, Massachusetts.